OLD SONGS IN A NEW CAFE

Also by Robert James Waller

The Bridges of Madison County
Slow Waltz in Cedar Bend
Images (photographs)

OLD SONGS
IN A
NEW CAFE

Autobiographical Stories by
Robert James Waller

HEADLINE

First published in 1994
by HEADLINE BOOK PUBLISHING
Published by arrangement
with Warner Books, Inc.

10 9 8 7 6 5 4 3 2 1

Excerpt from 'Memphis Tennessee' by Chuck Berry used with
permission from Chuck Berry and Isalee Music Publishing

Excerpt from the poem on page 51 from *Selected Poems of Rainer Maria
Rilke*, edited and translated by Robert Bly. Copyright © 1981 by Robert
Bly. Reprinted by permission of HarperCollins Publishers Inc.

The essays and stories have previously appeared in JUST BEYOND
THE FIRELIGHT, copyright © 1988 by Iowa State University Press;
ONE GOOD ROAD IS ENOUGH, copyright © 1990 by Iowa State
University Press; *The Des Moines Register, Country American, Humane
Society of the United States News, League Lines* and *Voice of Humanity*.
Publisher by arrangement with the Author and Iowa State University
Press, Ames

British Library Cataloguing in Publication Data

Waller, Robert James
Old Songs in a New Café
I. Title
813.54

ISBN 0-7472-1290-2

Printed and bound in Great Britain by
Mackays of Chatham PLC, Chatham, Kent

HEADLINE BOOK PUBLISHING
A division of Hodder Headline PLC
338 Euston Road
London NW1 3BH

FOR:

Georgia Ann, Rachael, Ruth, Robert, Sr.
Gerald, Charlie, Sammy, Roadcat
Perry, Harriet, Stan, Allen
And . . . Orange Band.

Acknowledgments

Thanks to Jim Flansburg, Jim Gannon, and Bill Silag, for their help and friendship, and for their support when others wavered. Thanks also to the Iowans who read what I wrote early on and encouraged me to write more. And, finally, thanks to the rivers (they know who they are) for being the source of it all.

Contents

Contents

Foreword

Essays by Robert James Waller began to appear in *The Des Moines Register* in 1983, but I did not encounter Waller's writing until 1986. That's when I read "Slow Waltz for Georgia Ann," a striking tribute to a romance still strong after thirty years, expressed with exceptional grace, dignity, and unabashed sincerity. It was rare to see such a thing in a newspaper—not only the subject matter but also the lyrical quality of the writing itself.

At the time, I was working as managing editor at Iowa State University Press, and in a letter I asked Waller about his writing plans and suggested that he and I discuss the possibility of publishing an autobiographical work that incorporated the pieces running in the *Register*. His response was cordial—and somewhat amused. An autobiography was probably a bit premature, he indicated, but the idea of an essay collection appealed to him. In fact, he was already at work on several additional *Register* pieces.

The following summer the *Register* published, in eight installments, Waller's magnificent account of an unaccompanied 100-mile journey he made by canoe on Iowa's Shell Rock River. The essay was at once a celebration of Iowa's natural beauty and an indictment of public indifference about its preservation. Waller's river voyage became the talk of Iowa and fueled debates in taverns and cafés across the state. Not everyone in Iowa was delighted by what Waller had written, but a flood of mail to the *Register* indicated Waller's message had been heard.

The mail also revealed the unusual appeal of the writer's style. It wasn't simply that Waller expressed people's concerns about the natural environment; it was the captivating way he said it. "You painted with words what I experienced, but found difficult to relate," wrote one reader.

Subsequent essays in the *Register* also drew praise, and increasingly readers' comments focused on Waller himself, rather than on his own subjects: "Some people are given the gift to be able to reach another person's heart," declared one letter, written in praise of "A Canticle for Roadcat." "You are loved and appreciated by a great number of people you probably will never meet, but who feel they know you because of a kindred spirit."

For some of us at least, discovering a writer like this can be a startling and even troubling experience—

here is someone giving candid expression to the vague longings stirring within us that we thought were only our own. Waller dares to describe these feelings, and does so with great skill. He draws us into his world with the elegance of his language and holds us there by the authority with which he addresses matters of concern to us all.

These are often matters of the heart, as in *The Bridges of Madison County* and in several of the essays collected here, often involving characters and situations having counterparts in our own lives. Especially in the earlier essays, Waller focuses on the events of a conventional midwestern life—a man and his family, his memories of childhood, and his concerns about the future. Yet even when he writes of experiences we know firsthand, Waller illuminates them so brilliantly that we are forced to look at things—memories and desires, families and relationships, landscapes—in new ways.

This isn't Waller's main purpose in writing. For him, the creative process is a personal exercise in self-discovery. "I am discovering, as I write, what I really think, what I really believe," he explains in his essay "Getting the Words Rightly Set." This is the magic— and the power—of creative writing as a means of self-expression. "Your deepest feelings can cause you to shudder a bit . . . because you didn't know they were there and writing has uncovered them."

But no matter what his topic, Waller has the ability to make it his own, such is the confidence with which he writes. This too is an expression of self. "I'm not refined and tentative as a person. I have strong emotions, I am passionate about things, I am a little rough around the edges, I can easily become overly sentimental, and all of this comes through in my writing," he said in a letter to me when we were just getting to know each other. And, he suggested, for him the outcome was perhaps less important than the process itself: "I take chances. . . . Sometimes things work out, sometimes they don't."

Things have worked out very well in the years since then. Eventually Waller published two books of essays with Iowa State University Press: *Just Beyond the Firelight* (1988) and *One Good Road Is Enough* (1990). Word of the two books spread gradually beyond Iowa, due in part to the reprinting of individual essays in national magazines but also as a result of Waller's own travels. Mail arriving at our offices and at Waller's home indicated that pockets of Waller fans had formed in Washington, New Mexico, and elsewhere around the country. Now of course what were once scattered fans are part of a network of Waller readers who have kept *The Bridges of Madison County* at the top of the best-seller lists for nearly a year.

Robert Waller's enormous popular success is a testament to his ability to draw readers into his quest for self-discovery. Recently Oprah Winfrey described *The Bridges of Madison County* as a book "that's touching souls all across the country." She told her television audience that when she finished the book, she wanted to talk to others who had read it and to share Waller's gift. Readers of the essays collected here are likely to react the same way, as they discover the distinctive gifts of a remarkable writer.

BILL SILAG
Iowa State University Press
January 1994

Preface

I began writing these little pieces on a warm, green morning in the summer of 1983. "Ridin' Along in Safety with Kennedy and Kuralt" was the first. Until then I had written only academic journal articles plus a fair number of songs I played and sang during my twenty-four years as a bar musician. Just why I decided to take up the writer's trade is not clear to me now, nor was it any clearer then, I suspect. In fact, until recently I'd never considered writing as a way to make a living. So, as best I remember, it merely seemed like an interesting thing to do at the time. I began writing for that reason and none other, which is pretty much the way I've lived my entire life.

I puttered along, writing mostly on weekends, publishing a few pieces each year in *The Des Moines Register*. People wrote or called to say they enjoyed the essays. Jim Gannon and Jim Flansburg of the *Register* encouraged me to keep writing. Since I was a university dean at the time, applause from anybody, anywhere, was welcome.

After reading "Slow Waltz for Georgia Ann," Bill Silag, who was then editor at the Iowa State University Press, suggested a collection of the *Register* pieces. That also seemed like a good thing to do, and it delighted me to think the essays would be gathered into a single volume, which we titled *Just Beyond the Firelight*. Taken together, they formed something of an autobiographical sketch covering my first forty years, and that sounded a whole lot easier than someday possibly writing a history of my meandering life for possible grandchildren who possibly might not care in any case.

A second collection, *One Good Road Is Enough*, was subsequently published, and suddenly I had two books in print when I never expected to have any. I began work on a third, which eventually appeared as *Iowa: Perspectives on Today and Tomorrow*, a fairly long and analytical work on the curious place of my growing and living.

Then came *The Bridges of Madison County*. To date, it has sold more than 4.5 million copies, has been on the *New York Times* best-seller list for 76 weeks, and has occupied the top position for 36 weeks. *Bridges* changed my life in ways I still do not completely understand. In any case, I'm pleased that Warner Books decided to reissue the early essays. I think you'll find they have much the same flavor as *Bridges*.

If I were to write these pieces now, I would not handle them as I originally did, but I am unapologetic about the way they look and taste. They represent where I was at the time they were written, nothing more. We come, we do, we go, and I think we should not take ourselves more seriously than that.

You'll meet my wife, my daughter, and my old friend and colleague, Roadcat, who was as good and true a friend as anyone could wish for. And I'll take you back with me to the flatlands dust and heat of Rockford, Iowa, in the 1940s and 1950s. There, in a quiet, unobtrusive place between two rivers, I found heroes of a size that suited me. For example, Sammy Patterson, billiards master; Kenny Govro, cat fisherman; and Perry Burgess, who worked as a kiln stacker at the local brick-and-tile plant.

We'll ride along through Asian nights with Captain Charlie Uban, an Iowa boy who took C-47 cargo planes into territory where they were never meant to go, into the snow and wind of the southern Himalayas when the world had lost control. We'll fly yet another time, with a flock of Canada geese beating their way south through a midwestern blizzard, and we'll think about what it means to fly no more when we look through cage wire at a fellow named Orange Band, who was the last member of his species, resting there on his perch and perhaps contemplating what zero truly means.

There's more—things run amuck when river otters are turned loose in Iowa, and we'll look at the art and technique of the long-range jump shot. I coast by my fiftieth birthday and wonder about it, my father confronts an assault on his honesty, and I run into an extraordinary woman in the back country of Florida.

In short, this is a book about people and animals and things I care about. It's about growing up and showing your stuff, finding love, winning and losing, and getting older. It's about where I began and where I came to at a particular time in my life, as a person and as a writer. And I suppose it's also about where I'm headed, though I never seem to realize such things at the time. We come, we do, we go, and the doing can be a rather grand voyage if you don't panic and if you believe, as I believe, in magic and imagination and wizards who live along quiet country rivers.

ROBERT JAMES WALLER
Cedar Falls, Iowa
January 1994

OLD SONGS IN A NEW CAFE

Excavating
Rachael's Room

L ike some rumpled alien army awaiting marching orders, the brown trash bags hunker down on the patio in a column of twos. A hard little caravan are they, resting in sunlight and shadow and caring not for their cargos, the sweepings of childhood and beyond.

With her eighteenth birthday near, Rachael has moved to Boston, leaving her room and the cleaning of it to us.

Originally published in *The Des Moines Register*, September 22, 1985.

After conducting a one-family attempt at turning United Parcel Service into something resembling North American Van Lines, we gather by the front door early on a Sunday morning.

Beside the suitcases are stacked six boxes, taped and tied. In my innocence, I tap the topmost box and ask, "What are these?"

"That's the stuff I couldn't get in my suitcases last night; you guys can send it to me," she replies, rummaging through her purse. Out of habit, I begin a droning lecture on planning ahead, realize the futility of it, and am quiet.

She has a deep caring for the animals and purposely, we know, avoids saying good-bye to them, particularly the small female cat acquired during her stay at camp one summer, years ago.

The cat has shared her bed, has been her confidant and has greeted her in the afternoons when she returned from school. Good-bye would be too much, would bring overpowering tears, would destroy the blithe air of getting on with it she is trying hard to preserve.

We watch her walk across the apron of the Waterloo airport, clutching her ticket, and she disappears into the funny little Air Wisconsin plane.

Turning, just as she left the departure lounge, she grinned and flashed the peace sign. I was all right until then, but with that last insouciant gesture, so typical of her, the poignancy of the moment is driven home and tears come.

We hurry outside and stand in hot sunlight to see

the plane leave. I note that we have never done this before, for anyone.

Clinging to the heavy fence wire along the airport boundary, I watch the plane take off to the west and make a last allegoric circle over Cedar Falls. East she travels and is gone, disappearing in the haze of an Iowa summer.

Back home, beer in hand, we sit on the porch, listening to the hickory nuts fall, recounting the failures and remembering the triumphs.

For the 500th time in the last eighteen years, we describe to each other the night of her birth, how she looked coming down the hall in the Bloomington, Indiana, hospital on the gurney in her mother's arms. How we felt, how we feel, what we did and didn't do.

We take a few days off, just to get used to the idea of there being only two of us again. Then, tentatively, we push open the door to her room.

The dogs peer into the darkness from around our legs and look up at us. The room—well—undulates. It stands as a shrine to questionable taste, a paean to the worst of American consumerism. The last few echoes of Def Leppard and Twisted Sister are barely audible. Georgia sighs.

I suggest flame throwers coupled with a front-end loader and caution the cleanup crew, which now includes the two cats, about a presence over in one of the corners. Faintly, I can hear it rustle and snarl. It is, I propose, some furry guardian of teenage values, and it senses, correctly, that we are enemies.

3

Trash bags in hand, we start at the door and work inward, tough-minded.

"My god, look at this stuff; let's toss it all."

The first few hours are easy. Half-empty shampoo bottles go into the bags, along with three dozen hair curlers, four dozen dried-up ball-point pens and uncountable pictures of bare-chested young men with contorted faces clawing at strange-looking guitars.

Farther into the room salvage appears: the hammer that disappeared years ago; about six bucks in change; 50 percent of the family's towel and drinking-glass stock; five sets of keys to the Toyota. More. Good stuff. We work with a vengeance.

Moving down through the layers, though, we begin to undergo a transformation.

Slowly, we change from rough-and-tumble scavengers to gentle archaeologists. Perhaps it started when we reached the level of the dolls and stuffed animals. Maybe it was when I found "The Man Who Never Washed His Dishes," a morality play in a dozen or so pages, with her childhood scribblings in it.

In any case, tough-mindedness has turned to drippy sentimentality by the time we find the tack and one shoe from Bill, her horse.

I had demanded that Bill be sold when he was left unridden after the five years of an intense love affair with him were over. That was hard on her, I know. I begin to understand just how hard when Georgia discovers a bottle of horsefly repellent that she kept for her memories.

We hold up treasures and call to each other. "Look at this, do you remember . . . ?"

And there's Barbie. And Barbie's clothes. And Barbie's camper in which the young female cat was given grand tours of the house, even though she would have preferred not to travel at all, thank you.

My ravings about the sexist glorification of middle-class values personified by Barbie seem stupid and hollow in retrospect, as I devilishly look at the cat and wonder if she still fits in the camper. "Here kitty, kitty . . ." Ken is not in sight. Off working out on the Nautilus equipment, I suppose. Or studying tax shelters.

Ah, the long-handled net with which Iowa nearly was cleared of fireflies for a time. "I know they look pretty in the bottle, Sweetheart, but they will die if you keep them there all night."

Twister—The Game That Ties You Up in Knots. The ball glove. She was pretty decent at first base. And the violin. Jim Welch's school orchestra was one of the best parts of her growing years.

She smiles out at us from a homecoming picture, the night of her first real date. Thousands of rocks and seashells. The little weaving loom on which she fashioned pot holders for entire neighborhoods. My resolve is completely gone as I rescue Snoopy's pennant from the flapping jaws of a trash bag and set it to one side for keeping.

We are down to small keepsakes and jewelry. Georgia takes over, not trusting my eye for value, and sorts the precious from the junk, while I shuffle through old algebra papers.

Night after night, for a year, I sat with her at the kitchen table, failing to convince her of the beauty to be found in quadratic equations and other abstractions. I

5

goaded her with Waller's Conjecture: "Life is a word problem." Blank stare.

Finally, trying to wave hope in the face of defeat, I paraphrased Fran Lebowitz: "In the real world, there is no algebra."

She nodded, smiling, and laughed when I admitted that not once, in all my travels, had I ever calculated how long Smith would need to overtake Brown if Brown left three hours before Smith on a slower train. I told her I'd sit in the bar and wait for Smith's faster train.

That confirmed what she had heretofore only suspected—algebra is not needed for the abundant life, only fast trains and good whiskey. And, she was right, of course.

The job is nearly finished. All that remains is a bit of archiving.

I have strange feelings, though. Have we sorted carefully enough? Probably. Georgia is thorough about that kind of thing. Still, I walk to the road again and look at the pile. The tailings of one quarter of a life stacked up in three dozen bags. It seems like there ought to be more.

When I hear the garbage truck, I peer out of an upstairs window in her room. The garbage guys have seen lives strung out along road edges before and are not moved. The cruncher on the truck grinds hair curlers and Twister and junk jewelry and broken stuffed animals— and some small part of me.

She calls from Boston. A *job*. Clerking in a store, and she loves it. We are pleased and proud of her. She's under way.

The weeks go by. Letters. "I am learning to budget my money. I hate it. I want to be rich."

She starts her search for the Dream in a rooming house downtown and finds a Portuguese boyfriend, Tommy, who drums in a rock band and cooks Chinese for her. Ella Fitzgerald sings a free concert in the park. The cop on the beat knows her, and the store is crowded with returning college kids late in a Boston summer. Here in the woods, it's quieter now.

Her room has been turned into a den. A computer replaces curling irons and other clutter on her desk. My pinstripes look cheerless in her closet where pink fishnet tops and leather pants once hung.

Order has replaced life. I sit quietly there and hear the laughter, the crying, the reverberation of a million phone calls. The angst of her early-teen existential crisis lingers, drifting in a small cloud near the high ceiling.

And you know what I miss? Coming home and hearing her say, "Looking pretty good, Bob! Got your suspenders on?" She could make a whirring sound just like the motor drive on a fine camera.

Those few moments of irreverent hassle every day are what I miss most of all.

Regrets? A few. I wish I had walked in the woods more with her. I wish I had gotten mad less and laughed longer. Maybe we could have kept the horse another year.

Victories? A few. She loves the music and the animals. She understands romance and knows how to live a romantic life. She also has the rudimentary skills of a great blackjack dealer. I sent her off with that instead of luggage.

She has her own agenda. She's had it for years. It's not my agenda, not what I would choose, but then she has more courage than I do. She's out there on her own, cooking on a hot plate in a Boston rooming house, pushing and shoving and working and discovering. My respect for her escalates. She's going to be all right.

And I know I'll sit on the porch as autumn comes this year and other years, in some old sweater with some old dreams, and wonder where she goes and how she goes.

I hope she goes where there's laughter and romance, and walks the streets of Bombay and leans out of Paris windows to touch falling January snow and swims in the seas off Bora Bora and makes love in Bangkok in the Montien Hotel.

I hope she plays blackjack all night in the Barbary Coast and, money ahead, watches the sun come up in Vegas. I hope she rides the big planes out of Africa and Jakarta and feels what it's like to turn for home just ahead of winter.

Go well, Rachael Elizabeth, my daughter. And, go knowing that your ball glove hangs on the wall beside mine, that Snoopy's pennant flies bravely in the old airs of your room, that the violin is safe, and that the little cat now sleeps with us at night but still sits on the porch railing in the late afternoon and looks for you.

Slow Waltz
for Georgia Ann

I hear the slap of the clay as you work it, late in the night. And I know you are there in your studio, in bib overalls, an old sweater, and heavy work shoes. Soon your wheel will begin to turn in time with some faint and distant music, and the teapots and lamps and goblets will lift effortlessly from nothing more than moistened earth.

So the night wind moves the trees outside, and I remember you from a college-town party hall. Twenty-

Originally published in *The Des Moines Register*, July 27, 1986.

eight years ago now. Through the smoke and across the tables we were taken with each other from the start. An enchanted evening. Our own private cliché. The sort of thing people don't believe in anymore.

And then years later I watch you. Coming toward me on your dancer's walk through the early twilight of high-plateau India. Your sari is silk, and blue above your sandals, your earrings are gold and dangling long. Heads above bodies in white wicker chairs along the veranda of the West End Hotel turn as you pass. Your already dark skin has been made even darker from our days in the Bangalore sun, and there are speculations about you. An Indian man asks, "Is she Moroccan?" "No," I reply. "She is Iowan."

I take another beer from the refrigerator, hoping you stay in your studio a while longer. I want to sit here by myself, listening to the muffled sounds of your hands at work, and think about what it means to be married to you for twenty-five years. In another month, it will have been that long.

I grew up dreaming of rivers and music and ancient cities and dark-haired women who sang old songs in cafés along the Seine. You were raised to be a wife and a beauty, and you probably would have been satisfied, maybe happier, with a more conventional man. At least it took you a long time to discover what I am up to and to know this race I run, a race between death and discovery. You were plainly discomfited by my lurching from one passion to another, from basketball to music, from the academy to think tanks, from city to city, from the solitude of my study to the dark bars where I am at home with my instruments.

Early on, with me dancing along early morning beaches and feeding my demons, it was clear that you would need a life of your own if this marriage were to flourish. That was your hardest struggle. It almost broke us apart. But you found something in the clay, something that quietly said, "This is me."

And I knew we had won when the woman at the cocktail party gushed: "Oh, you must be the potter's husband!" Inside of me, at that moment, I shouted in celebration. Not for myself, or even for us, but for you. Chrysalis had died, you had become. Now the potter's work and the potter's trade keep you centered like the clay.

Love? I cannot analyze that. It is of a piece. Taken apart, it becomes something else, and the gull-like melody that is ours disappears. But even in our difficult times, times when we took suitcases down from closet shelves and stared at each other in anger, love was there.

Liking is another matter. I can get a hold on that. Most of all, I think, I like you for the good-natured understanding you worked so hard to acquire, even if that understanding sometimes borders on wavering tolerance.

You understand the need to live with old furniture and rusted cars and only two kitchen cabinets and rough wooden floors and vacuum cleaners that don't vacuum and clothes washers that operate correctly only when the tab from a beer can is stuck just so behind the dial, so that a little money will be there when I yell over the side of the loft, "Let's go to Paris!"

11

Remember the time I was in graduate school and we had less than $100 in the bank, when I considered trading our doddering Volkswagen for a guitar? You crinkled your face, looked serious, and said, with no hint of the scold, "How will we get to the grocery store?" You said only that. And I was grateful.

You tolerate one side of the living room stacked with music equipment, while my canoe full of camping gear and two cats tenants the other side, stretching from one corner over to where it inelegantly mingles with an amplifier, several microphone stands, and old suitcases full of cords and other necessary truck. I am working on the gunnels and mumbling about river maps I can't find and rotten weather and wizards I am going out to search for. Over dinner, you smile softly and ask, "How long do you think the canoe will be in the living room?" The point is made. I will move it out tomorrow. Or maybe the day after.

You are older now. I can see that if I look hard. But I don't. I have always seen you in soft focus. I see you standing in the winter on a great stretch of deserted beach in the Netherlands Antilles brushing your long and freshly washed hair in the sea wind from Venezuela. I see you in khaki and sandals at the waterfront café in French Marigot listening to an island band play a decent imitation of vintage American rock 'n' roll. Chuck Berry and ol' Jerry Lee were part of our courting years, and we grin at the aging lyrics—"Long distance information, give me Memphis, Tennessee. . . ."

I glance over and see you beside me at blackjack tables around the world. Was it in Vegas where you wore a long gold dress and the fur coat you bought for $50 at a second-hand clothing shop? I think so. We played all night, I remember that. Guilty though you felt about buying anything made of fur, you were the perfect 1930s vamp as I counted cards in my blue suspenders.

Or I look up ever so slightly from the fingerboard of my jazz guitar and watch as you play the second chorus of "Gone with the Wind," the one where you do the little two-fingered runs I like so well. You are hunched over the keyboard, lightly swaying in pink and white and wearing dark glasses. The sun hammers down, while people dance, by a pool, on the Fourth of July, in Chicago.

And you are sleepy in bed and lit so gently by early light when I bring you coffee on high, hard winter mornings, while the wood stove putters around trying to douse the cold of the night. I have been up for hours reading and writing. You are no morning person, so talk must come later. Still, I hover around, clumsily, just to look at you and smell the warm, perfumed scent of your body.

It seems I have spent a lifetime running toward you. I have tossed in my bed in Arabian desert towns and wanted you. I have stared off midnight balconies in deep Asia, watching dhows older than me tug at their moorings and long for the thrash of coastal waters, missing you and wondering about you.

I am uneasy at being nearly thirty-hours' flying time from you. That's too far. Then, over the miles and across the oceans, through a thousand airports, I am home, wrinkled and worn, and you are there with a single rose and a small sign that says, "Welcome Home, Captain

13

Cook, Welcome Home." Late into the night we laugh as I take the gold and silver presents from my battered suitcase.

I have trusted the years, and I was right to do so. They brought me you. We have watched others' lives intertwine and then unravel. But we have held together. At least for this life, in this time.

Yet I am haunted by the feeling that we might not meet again, that this might be just our one moment in the great sweep of things. Once, as I lay on the floor, breathing through oxygen tubes, looking past the somber faces of paramedics, I saw your tears, and I felt a great sadness, worrying not about myself, but rather that I might not find you again in the swirling crowds out there in the centuries to come. It was the loss of you, not life, that I feared.

For we have come by different ways to this place. I have no feeling that we met before. No déjà vu. I don't think it was you in lavender by the sea as I rode by in A.D. 1206 or beside me in the border wars. Or there in the Gallatins, a hundred years ago, lying with me in the silver-green grass above some mountain town. I can tell by the natural ease with which you wear fine clothes and the way your mouth moves when you speak to waiters in good restaurants. You have come the way of castles and cathedrals, of elegance and empire.

If you were there in the Gallatins, you were married to a wealthy rancher and lived in a grand house. I was a gambler at the table or the mountain man at the bar or the fiddler in the corner, playing a slow waltz to his memories. The dust from your carriage was of more value than my life in those days, and it drowned me in longing and sullied my dreams as you passed by in the street. Somehow, though, for this life and this time, we came together. You taught me about caring and softness and intimacy. The task before me was to teach you about music. And dreams. And how to savor the smell of ancient cities and the sound of cards whispering across green felt. This I have done.

So I rest secure knowing that you have learned and that, in another time, you might recognize me coming across the street of some gambler's town, in high brown boots with an old fiddle case over my shoulder, as your carriage moves by in the dust. And perhaps you will smile and nod and, for a strange and flickering moment, you will remember how the waves of January wash the sea wall at Marigot.

Incident at
Sweet's Marsh

I can get excited about river otters. They not only look neat, they also are among those of God's creatures who take play seriously. If they were human, they'd probably live in California, drive Porsches, and have something to do with the entertainment business.

So it was that my heart fairly leapt when I read the announcement in *The Des Moines Sunday Register*. It said that twenty river otters would be released the following

Originally published in *The Des Moines Register*, April 27, 1988.

Wednesday at Sweet's Marsh, near Tripoli. I organized my week around that event, packed a sandwich and my cameras, and left for Tripoli early on a bright March morning.

I figured the crowd at the release would be small—a few people from the Iowa Department of Natural Resources with the animals and maybe a half-dozen other grizzled outdoor types. After all, I spend days along the rivers of Iowa without seeing anyone other than profiles in cars going over bridges.

When I pulled into the access to Sweet's Marsh, a man wearing a camouflage shirt said I should continue straight ahead for parking instructions. I always listen to men wearing camouflage shirts, no matter what they are telling me, so I continued on and parked behind eight other cars on the shoulder of the road. No one was there to provide parking instructions, so, as typical Iowans, we just worked it out for ourselves.

It was at this point I began to experience a slight twitching in my stomach, and it had nothing to do with the coffee in my thermos. You see, I never go to any place where parking instructions are required. That stems from multiple traumatic experiences I had as a child when Jaycees wearing pith helmets and waving canes used to direct traffic at the county fair. I began to associate parking instructions with crowds and noise and other assaults on my tender sensibilities.

By 9 A.M., approximately sixty people had gathered and were surrounding two small cages containing a few otters for public display. People stood around commenting about the animals' inherent cuteness and firing away with point-and-shoot cameras.

"Well, this isn't too bad," I thought. Then I saw the state trooper. I also never go to events where state troopers are required. Not because I don't like state troopers, understand. My experiences with them have been distant, but pleasant. It's just that the presence of a trooper meant that crowd control of a somewhat higher order might be required.

I moved off to one side, poured a little coffee into my cup, and considered it all. Meanwhile, the DNR folks were busy stringing rope barricades along the south side of the inlet where the otters would be released. I started adding it up: parking instructions plus state trooper plus rope barricades equals *uh oh*.

But I love otters and wanted to see the little folks out of their wire mesh cages and in the water. So I decided to grit it out. That was when the yellow school buses began to arrive, and I knew it was all over.

I absolutely never go anywhere that involves yellow school buses. Never. Unless I am paid, and paid handsomely, for it. But the buses came and purged themselves of their cargos. The running, jumping, shrieking future business leaders of America poured from the open doors, glands pounding. But, what the hell. It's better than another hour of Cooperative Living (For Seniors Only, Elective) taught from some smarmy textbook designed to kill creative passion once and for all.

The students ran to be in the front row behind the rope barricades. I ran to the north side of the inlet where I figured the swampy ground would discourage those in new Reeboks. No luck. I had merely broken the ice by being the first into that area. Another veteran of

19

the rivers soon joined me, grumbling about what a mess this was turning out to be.

Then came a heavy-set guy pawing through the branches with a 35-mm camera equipped with at least a 14,000-mm lens. That not being enough, he had affixed a teleconverter between the lens and the camera, which increases the effective length of the lens. He was hand-holding the camera and lens and attachments. I lost track of him, but if he was able to avoid sinking in the lowland low and to lift the apparatus to eye level and fire, I can tell you what his pictures look like without seeing them. It's the way the world looks to someone who has just been hit sharply behind the ear with a tire iron.

More yellow school buses. Driven by the same drivers, of course. I finally sorted it all out a few years ago. There are only twelve school bus drivers in the whole world. That's why they all seem to look the same.

I staked out a couple of feet of ground, set up my tripod, and asked the ninth-grade boys behind me to please stop pushing each other into the tree branch that whacked me each time one of them fell against it. Why do ninth-grade boys always push each other? Why haven't we shipped them all to North Dakota until they calm down?

By this time, I knew exactly why the state trooper was there. He had a drawn and jaundiced look to him, a legacy of too many county fairs and otter releases. I estimated the crowd at four hundred, with more cars and buses still arriving. At 9:30, the promised time for the freeing of the otters, a Department of Natural Resources man with a new-age bullhorn got on top of a pickup truck and asked the crowd for its attention. Attention? He had to be kidding.

Then he started a spiel about otters and their habitat and how lucky we are to have seed stock that may result in a viable otter population in Iowa. He tried to point out that we used to have lots of otters, but that they were driven to extinction by pollution, loss of habitat, and yellow school buses.

His speech did not go well. It suffered the same problems as 98.73 percent of all other speeches—an inadequate sound system and length. It went something like this: "Baarraak . . . otters . . . (muffled words) . . . rrarkk . . . thanks to . . . kkkzzrrak."

He did manage somehow to get across that it would take decades before the otter population was large enough to "harvest." There's that word again! We persist in using the euphemism wherever the slaughtering of attractive animals is being talked about. Dammit, we kill them. We slaughter them, just like we slaughter cattle. We catch them in steel traps or blow them down with shotguns. We rip off their hides and wear their furs or hang their heads on den walls. We *kill them*, we don't *harvest them*! Someday we'll all grow up and face that reality.

The speech droned on and on, the crowd became restive. You could almost hear it under people's breath—a chant still in the mind but ready to spring forth if the speech continued. "We want the otters, we want the otters, we want. . . ." The state trooper stiffened, sensing the otter-release equivalent of a feeding frenzy.

But I don't blame the DNR people. Cripes, they

spend most of their time in obscurity, working hard with seines and handling squishy, crawly things under an August sun. By jove, for once they had a crowd, and this was a chance for their message to get across, whatever it was.

While the speaker spoke, other DNR personnel dragged several of the cages full of squirming otters down close to the water. And, of course, the media photographers with their usual, but unwarranted, privileges crowded around with whirring gizmos and other gear, blocking the view of those who had come to see the otters. It was worth thirty-three seconds on the evening news, I later noticed.

Braced, feet wide apart, I protected my Nikon from the high school boys on my left who had never seen a camera before and insisted on standing in front of it. They could be dealt with, though.

The real problem came from the five-year-old boy on my right who discovered that if you stamp your feet hard in the water, the water flies in all directions. I asked him to stop and pointed at the drops of water on my camera equipment. He ran behind his father's pant leg a few feet away.

The DNR speaker shouted something about how the school buses would be organized to pick up the masses after the event. Personally, I thought the DNR ought to unfurl one of its large river seines, pull it through the crowd, and drag the lot of us all the way to Tripoli. I loved the image, dwelt on it.

The moment was near, I thought. I couldn't be sure, since the media photographers were practically riding the cages as they were moved nearer the water. But, here and there, I got a glimpse of brown fur in the morning sun, and this fur seemed to be moving toward the quiet water of Sweet's Marsh.

I crouched behind my tripod and concentrated on focusing the Nikon. Wham! The five-year-old boy I sent away three minutes ago was back. He had discovered that if you smash the water with a stick, the water flies all over everything. I straightened up, tapped the short-bladed hunting knife that is a standard part of my outdoor kit, and said in a low baritone, "Swamp devil die young."

I wiped the water from my camera, while the kid disappeared toward his father. Ready now, here they come. One of the cages was opened, and three otters waddled toward the water. After that, it was bedlam.

The otters swam through the water, ran along the banks, and wrestled with one another in grass and sunshine. More otters were shown the water, and they knew what to do with it. The DNR man with the bullhorn shouted something about "rotating the crowd so everyone can see the otters." Nobody paid him any mind. Instead they slithered under the rope barricade and plunged toward the banks of Sweet's Marsh.

The program was just getting under way, but I packed my gear and walked to the car. I'll go back on some cold, rainy day in autumn, a few months from now. I judge it will take that long to get the ninth-grade boys back in their cages and for the yellow school buses to get loaded and back to Tripoli.

What can be concluded from this event? First, I'm glad the river otters are back in Iowa, and the people responsible for this are to be applauded without end. I truly mean that. I am amplified in spirit just knowing the otters are out there giving it a try.

Second, if I were a political candidate, I'd use my campaign contributions to corner the market on river otters and prodigiously announce the times and locations of their releases. Then, I'd get a sound system that works; I'd tell everybody how much I love river otters; I'd promise that we will never kill them, especially the babies. Furthermore, I'd promise that we will add more school bus drivers to supplement the existing twelve and that all books dealing with cooperative living will be burned at Sweet's Marsh as a testament to free speech. I'd be elected president of the galaxy.

Finally, in light of all the fun we had with the otter release at Sweet's Marsh, I'm rethinking some of my earlier recommendations about Iowa developing a tourist industry.

A Canticle for Roadcat

I had a friend ... and his name was Roadcat. He was young when I was young and old when I was middle-aged. Still, our lives overlapped for a while, and I am grateful for that.

He was more than a friend, really. Friend and colleague is perhaps a better image. In fact, I sometimes introduced him to strangers as my research associate. We worked together on cold, gray afternoons, poring over

Originally published in *The Des Moines Register*, February 14, 1988.

25

books and papers, while the wood stove quietly crackled its way through another Iowa winter.

Sometimes he lay upon my lap and served as a round and honest book rest. He purred and occasionally reached out to turn pages for me, randomly and with a keen appreciation of the virtues surrounding leisurely scholarship. In the spring, as the days warmed, he moved to the desk, clearing a place for himself by pushing to the floor paper, pens, staplers, and other implements of a writer's trade.

He came from a field of long grass behind our house in Columbus, Ohio. Just a few inches in length, he walked along the cement of one of those smarmy subdivisions that make your teeth curl.

A neighbor's child abused him. He fought back, as any of us would, and the child's mother screamed something about rabid cats. My wife observed that the child deserved something more than he got and brought the kitty home for the customary saucer of milk.

I set him on my lap and said, "This is going to be a fine-looking cat." But we were on the move in those times and had already promised our daughter one of the kittens from a litter down the street. So the migrant was fed and sent along.

I sat down to read the paper, glanced up, and he had reappeared on the opposite side of the house at the patio screen door. He looked in at me, and I looked back. He coughed continuously and badly, tried to cry, but the effort was soundless. I picked him up, looked him over with a modest expertise gained from years of living around animals, and said I was taking him to the veterinarian's office.

The examination was lengthy. He had worms, ear mites, fleas, and a serious case of bronchitis. I asked the vet, "Is this a road cat?" The doctor smiled, "This is your genuine road cat."

We drove home together, he and I and, of course, four kinds of medicine in a brown paper bag. He sat on the car seat, small and uncomplaining, watching me, bright face hopeful. The nursery opened. Roadcat had come to stay.

And it is here, before going on, that I must deal with the issue of sentimentality. If I do not come to grips with that, you might dismiss the rest of what I have to say as mawkish and lacking sound perspective.

Humans have an arrogant manner of ranking life, as if some squat, three-level hierarchy of existence were fact instead of intellectual artifice. God by various names is way up there, of course, in the first position. A little further down, just a little, lies humankind. Below that, and far below, according to common belief, rests a great squishy level of everything else. Here, we find plants and animals. Maybe even rivers and mountains.

All right, let's admit that some transcending presence roams above us. Some call it God, some call it science. Others of us see it as a design so perfect, a great swirling form of truth and beauty and justice and balance, that cosmic ecology might be our term.

That leaves us and the rest. And if you're going to attempt rankings, you better have some criteria, some standards of measurement, to use in making your judgments. The problem is that we humans generate the criteria by which the rankings are made. That's letting the fox in with the chickens, or the cat in with the canary, or us in with beauty. Take your choice.

I read the philosophers sometimes. They have criteria, such as consciousness and the ability to use technology, for determining who and what get to belong to various communities. But I do not trust their judgments, for the reason just mentioned. I prefer to think of civilizations that are, well, just different—separate, but parallel and equal.

And I don't spend much time trying to create workable taxonomies either. Others do that sorting rather competently. But taxonomies always end up looking like hierarchies, and things eventually get a little too classified for my taste.

So I just coast along with the notion of parallel civilizations. It works pretty well for me. Bears and butterflies, trees and rivers. I try to live alongside rather than above them. Our world is fashioned to make this difficult, but I try.

Those of you who see things differently, as a matter of "better than" or "on a higher plane than," are to be pitied. I'm sorry to be so blunt, but I know your view is only one way, and that is down. As such, you miss the grand vistas, the shuddering sense of wonderment that comes from looking out across all the civilizations riding along together on Eddington's great arrow of time.

And so it was with my friend Roadcat. Riding

along on the arrow, we turned the days and marked the pages together. We grinned at each other over sunny afternoons on the deck, and, while he rested in the crook of my folded arm, we tilted our furry heads and stared high and hard at the lights of space just before dawn. Green eyes looking. Blue eyes looking. Wondering about ourselves and the others out there looking back.

We did that for twelve years plus a month or so. And we came to care, and care deeply, one for the other. He clearly saw, as I eventually did, that power and exploitation were not part of the reflections from each other's eyes. We came to a position of trust, and, in his wisdom and elegance, that was all he asked.

I violated that trust only once. I must take time to tell you about it, for the event contains the thread of a hard lesson.

Roadcat represented all the classic definitions of beauty and good taste. The long, soft pelage on his back and sides was predominantly black and gray. His chin was an off-white that flowed into creamy tan along his chest and belly. Symmetrically perfect were his markings, and he watched his world through green eyes of great immensity and color. His face was expressive, his conformation perfect.

Given that, it becomes understandable why we fell into the snare of seeing him as an object. When the local cat fanciers association announced a show limited to animals of something called pet quality, we could not resist.

So Roadcat was put into a wire cage and carried off to the show held as part of the Cattle Congress festivi-

29

ties in Waterloo. Along with the sheep and horses and cattle and hogs, the pet-quality cats would have their day in the ring. He was terrified and panting as I carried him through the crowds, past the Ferris wheel and midway barkers, past Willie Nelson's touring bus.

Roadcat's world was the forest, the warm place under the wood stove, and a canvas deck chair in the summer. He was content with himself and required no conspicuous recognition to prove his worth. His colleague apparently did require it. My wife, my daughter, and I wore blue T-shirts we had made up for the occasion that said "Roadcat" in bold, black letters across the front.

I watched him closely in the great hall where the judging was held. He was restless in the cage. Finally, he simply lay down and stared directly at me, straight in the eyes. I could see he was disappointed with me, and I was ashamed at having so ruthlessly shattered our mutual respect. Since a time when I was quite young, I have been angered by those public adulations of the human form called beauty contests, and here I was subjecting my friend to exactly that.

Roadcat refused to be an object. Normally temperate and reserved around strangers, he tore at the paper lining his cage on the judging platform, attempted to push his way through the metal top of his containment, and, when the judge put him on a table for all to see, he simply slid onto his back and tried to scratch the well-meaning woman who was to measure his worth.

Suddenly, confusion erupted among the various judges and assistants. A huddle formed around Roadcat, and I went forward to see what was happening. One of the assistant judges had lodged a complaint, contending that Roadcat was a purebred and did not belong in a pet-quality show. The supreme arbiter was consulted, and her verdict was this: Roadcat was the prototype image of a breed called Maine coon cats, descendants of random matings between domestic cats who rode the sailing ships from Europe and wild cats of the New World.

In the American cat shows of the late nineteenth century, the Maine coon cats were the most treasured breed of all. The head judge explained that if this had been 1900, Roadcat would have been the perfect specimen.

But humans are never satisfied with nature, and the Maine coon cats, for reasons not clear to either Roadcat or me, had been bred over the decades to have longer noses. Thus Roadcat was held to be something of a relic, slightly out of date, and was allowed in the show.

He scored high on appearance. The judge said, "He has a wonderful coat, a beautiful face, and the largest, prettiest green eyes I have ever seen." But, sliding and fighting and slashing out for the nearest human jugular vein within reach, he received a failing grade on the personality dimension and was awarded a fourth-place ribbon. Those green eyes brimmed with nasty satisfaction when the judge said, "I'll bet he's not like this at home, is he?"

Back through the midway, past the Ferris wheel, past Willie Nelson's bus, and home to the woods. He was disinterested in his remarkable heritage, slept away his terror, and had nothing to do with any of us for some

31

time. Gradually, he accepted my apologies, and our friendship warmed. But he made me work on re-crafting our trust as though it were a fine piece of furniture.

Roadcat was good-natured about most things, though, and seemed to enjoy the little inanities we created around his presence. On pasta nights, his name was changed temporarily to Roadicotta. When my wife, Georgia, held her seasonal pottery sales at our home, he charmed the customers by finding a large pot in which to sit and look out at the commotion. He became "The Retailer" on those occasions. He was "The Chief Inspector" for anything new that came into the house or onto the property, including musical instruments, canoes, and furnaces. In his later years, we called him "The Old Duffer" or "The Big Guy." But mostly he went by Roadie.

He even tolerated the nonsense of my singing songs appropriate to the can of food he and I chose each morning. Seafood Supper? I sang a verse of an old whaling song to the pitch of the electric can opener. How about Country Style for Cats? That got him "San Antonio Rose" in B-flat major, and Elegant Entré was served with a sprinkling of Cole Porter.

The undergrowth and woodland trails around our house were Roadcat's beat. He was a hunter, but not a killer. Now and then smaller creatures died from fright or the initial pounce when he caught them, yet I never saw him intentionally kill anything. Not even the night crawlers he brought to me after heavy rains. He plopped them down on a small throw rug, flipped it over to hamper their escape, and seemed pleased with himself.

The chipmunk was very much alive in the summer of 1986 when Roadie strolled through the front door and dropped it. The little guy hit the carpet running, dashed through a pile of old magazines, and disappeared in the general vicinity of the fireplace.

Judging that the chipper would not eat much, I was content to let him stay. The rest of the family, as usual, thought I was deranged. So, after four days of moving furniture, we flushed the poor fellow. The male dog nailed him to the floor in one of those wild scenes that seem to occur only at our house in the woods. Roadcat watched the entire battle with detached interest. Revenge for the cat-show humiliation finally was his.

In his habits he was careful, in his ways he was gentle. He found our dogs inelegant to the point of being despicable, but he liked the little female kitty that came along some years after he joined the craziness that is ours. He smiled tolerantly when she tried to nurse him and, through the years, gently washed her with a pink and tireless tongue.

Roadcat asked for little other than consideration and respect. He ate what was offered and left our food alone, except for my lunchtime glass of milk resting unattended on the table. He could not resist that. Turning around, I would find him sitting by the glass, licking a milk-covered paw.

That was his only sin, and I reached a compromise with him on the matter by providing him occasionally with a little milk in an old jelly glass decorated with etchings of Fred Flinstone. I think Fred reminded him of earlier times, before humans developed the technology of killing to a high and ludicrous art, when his saber-toothed cousins left no doubt about the equality of things. When he thought of that delicious state of affairs, it made the milk taste even better, and he lingered over it, humming to himself about woodlands and cliffs and open meadows turning yellow in the light of a younger sun.

The early bronchitis had taken most of his voice. So when he wanted attention, he would lie on my computer printer while I typed, purr loudly, and look directly into my face. If that failed, he escalated his tactics by jumping into the box holding the printer paper and tearing it off the machine. Finally, if I was so insensitive as to further ignore his requirements, he would race around the house, across my desk, along the balcony railing, and, eventually, onto my lap. He seldom failed in these efforts.

I watched him turn a little more gray here and there, but I suppressed melancholy thoughts of the inevitable. Roadcat maintained a youngness of spirit and, even in his latter days, could race thirty feet up a tree on any crisp spring morning when he felt like doing so. Yet, as we read Barbara Tuchman's *Stilwell and the American Experience in China* together in the last months of his life, I could almost sense something as he purred his way through the pages. I would lift my eyes from the book, smile at him, and softly stroke his head, which he always acknowledged by a slight increase in the intensity of his purring.

In late September of 1987, I caught a slight hesitation in his leap to the basement table where I placed his food, safe from the growling hunger of the dogs. If I had not shared that breakfast time with him all those hundreds of mornings, I would not have noticed anything. But it was there—a slight, ever-so-slight, hesitation, as if he had to gather himself physically for what should have been an easy leap.

Simultaneously, he seemed to be eating a little less than was normal for him. The usual pattern was that he would eat about one-third of the can of food on the first serving. Then the female cat, who deferred to his seniority, took her turn. Later, Roadcat would come by and finish whatever was left.

But the rhythm faltered. There always was something in the dish at the end of the day. And sometimes he ate nothing after I ladled out the food. His face was thinning a bit, and his coat lost a little of its sheen.

I was about to make an appointment at the veterinarian's when one morning he did not appear for his dawn excursion. It was his custom to come lie near my pillow at first light and wait for me to rise and let him out. The routine was invariant, and the morning it was broken I felt an unpleasant twinge in my stomach.

I searched the house and found him lying in a chair in the back bedroom upstairs. I knelt down beside him, spoke softly, and ran my hand over his fur. He purred quietly, but something was not right.

While waiting for the vet's office to open, I remembered the previous evening. He had seemed strangely restless. He would get on my lap, then down again, then return for another cycle of the same thing. He did that five times, and I remarked to my wife that it was something of a record. The last time he walked up my chest and rubbed his cheek against mine. Though he

35

was always pleasantly affectionate, such a gesture was a little out of the ordinary. He was trying to tell me that something was amiss, that it was almost over.

The initial diagnosis was a kidney problem, which is not unusual in older animals. After a few days, we brought him home. He was terribly weak and could scarcely walk. I laid him on a wool poncho, where he stayed the entire night.

In the morning, I carried him to his litter box in the basement and set him down by it. He seemed disoriented and stumbled. I noticed his right leg was limp and curled underneath him when he sat.

Back to the doctor. An X-ray disclosed a large tumor around his heart, which had resulted in a stroke the previous night that paralyzed his right side and left him blind. Wayne Endres is a kind and patient man, but I could see he was working at the edge of his technology.

The following day, a Wednesday, Wayne called with his report. If it had only been a stroke, we might have worked our way out of it, even though cats don't recover from such things easily. But clearly, the tumor was large and growing, and there was little to be done. It was up to me, of course. But Wayne's quiet voice carried the overtones of despair when he said, "Roadcat is not doing well." He refused to offer hope. There wasn't any, and Wayne Endres is an honest man.

Here, at this point, the thunder starts, and civilizations that are normally parallel begin to intersect and become confused. Roadie and I shared a common language of trust, respect, and love, made visible by touching and aural by our private mutterings to one another. But, as it should be, the language of caring is a language of imprecision and is not designed for hard and profound choices.

I had no set of alternatives rich enough to evade the issue and none available that could even ameliorate it. And how could I understand what decision rules lay beating softly in the imprints of Roadcat's genetic spirals? For all I knew, they might be superior to mine, probably were, but I could not tell.

I know how I want to be treated under those dire conditions. But what right did I have to assume that so ancient a civilization as Roadcat's bears the same values as mine? How could I presume to judge when the standards are someone else's and I had not been told?

Surely, though, notions of dignity and suffering must be common to all that lives, whether it be rivers or butterflies or those who laugh and hold your hand and lie with you in autumn grass. So, gathering myself as best I could, I drove slowly through a red and yellow sunset toward Wayne Endres's clinic.

Someone once defined sentimentality as too much feeling for too small an event. But events are seldom small when you're dealing with civilizations. And they are never small when you're dealing with true companions.

My friend and colleague from all the years and gentle moments lay on a table with white cloth-like paper under him. I sat down, and at the sound and smell of me, he raised his head, straight up came his ears, and his nose wrinkled. Though the room was brightly lit, his brain kept sending a false message of darkness, and the pupils of his green eyes dilated to the maximum as he strained for the light.

He had lost half his body weight. I touched him along the neck, and there was a slight sound. He was trying to purr, but fluid in his throat would not allow it. Still, he wriggled his nose and tried to send all the old signals he knew I would recognize.

I nodded to Wayne and put my face next to that of my friend, trying somehow to convey the anguish I suffered for him and for myself, for my ignorance of right and wrong, and for my inability to know what he might want in these circumstances. I spoke softly to him, struggling with desperate intensity to reach far and across the boundaries of another nation, seeking either affirmation or forgiveness. When all that is linear failed me, I called down the old language of the forest and the plains to tell him, once and finally, of my gratitude for his simply having been.

And I wondered, as did S. H. Hay, "How could this small body hold/So immense a thing as death?"

Eventually, his head lowered, and it was done. Georgia and I carried him home in a blanket and buried him in the woods along one of the trails where he earned his living.

For some days after, I swore I would never go through that again. If it came to euthanasia, I would refuse to be present. I have changed my mind. You owe that much to good companions who have asked for little and who have traveled far and faithfully by your side.

Roadcat didn't just live with us. He was a spirited

participant in the affairs of our place. He was kind to us, and we to him. I remember, when I came home in the evenings, how he would move down the woodland path toward me, grinning, riding along on his little stiff-legged trot, tail held high with a slight curl at the tip. I'd hunker down, and we would talk for a moment while he rolled over on his back and looked at me, blinking.

Georgia and I put the shovel away, walked back into the darkness, and stood by the little grave. By way of a farewell, she said, "He was a good guy." Unable to speak, I nodded and thought she had said it perfectly. He was, indeed, a good guy. And a true friend and colleague who rode the great arrow with me for a time, helping me turn the pages in some old book while the wood stove quietly crackled its way through the winter afternoons of Iowa.

Romance

MR. PRESIDENT
MEMBERS OF THE PLATFORM PARTY
CANDIDATES FOR GRADUATION
FACULTY MEMBERS
PARENTS
LADIES AND GENTLEMEN

I t seems more than just a bit strange to be standing here today. It was in this very building, this room, that I received my B.A. degree in 1962. Prior to that event, however, I had spent an ungodly number of hours here in my wildly misspent youth. You see, I played basketball for what was then Iowa State Teachers College. For three years I ran all over this room in short pants, dribbling and shooting. I can still hear the

Commencement speech at the University of Northern Iowa, July 29, 1983. Originally published in *The Des Moines Register*, September 4, 1983.

41

voice of my late father as he sat along the sidelines over there and shouted words of encouragement as we battled the University of North Dakota or South Dakota State. He used to drive down from Rockford, Iowa, on cold winter nights and add his voice to the 4,000 students who invariably packed this place as we ran and jumped our way through season after season. My father always thought books could make you happier than basketballs. He was right. But that's another story for another time.

The point is, this place is filled with memories, and memories play an important part in what I want to talk about today. Since I am dean of the School of Business, I am absolutely sure a number of you turned out expecting to get some hot tips on microcomputer stocks or the latest news on money supply fluctuations. Sorry. Nor am I going to lecture you on (1) how well educated you are, (2) what wonderful opportunities you have before you, or (3) the importance of making great and lasting changes out there.

What I want to talk about is something a little different, something that makes all the living and doing you are so anxious to get on with worthwhile. More than that, it makes the living and doing better—better in terms of quality and quantity. I am going to talk about romance.

I looked up the definition of romance in several dictionaries. As I guessed, reading definitions of romance is about the most unromantic thing you can do. So I will not define romance, at least not directly. Rather, you will pick up a sense of what romance is by what I am going to say about it.

I am a musician and a writer of songs. One of my

songs, which I call "High Plains Afternoon," starts like this:

> *I see you now, as you were then,*
> *on a high plains afternoon.*
> *(Don't you remember the flowers,*
> *don't you remember the wind?)*
> *As naked you danced through the*
> *late autumn dust,*
> *while a threat of hard winter rode the cobalt horizon.*
> *(Don't you remember those who were free?*
> *We drove them out of our lives.)*

As I sing the song, it carries a sense that I am singing about a woman. Ostensibly I am. But it is also a song about the idea of romance, as she (pardon the gender) dances before us and then out of our lives, if we do not treat her right. Romance, you see, is something you have to take care of—romance needs food and water and care, of a kind all her own. You can destroy romance, or at least drive her away, almost without knowing that you are doing it. Let me give you an example.

A while back, a professor on this campus was finishing her doctorate. As part of her dissertation, she was conducting interviews with married folks about the subject of, well, marriage. When she asked Georgia Ann and me to participate, we thought it over. Then we politely said "no." Now, we have been married for almost twenty-two years, and a high level of zest remains in our relationship, so probably we have some useful things to say about marriage. Why did we decide not to? Because

43

we have agreed that too much analysis of certain things removes the romance from them. Our relationship is one of those things.

Romance dances just beyond the firelight, in the corner of your eye. She does not like you to look at her directly; she flees from the cold light of logic and data collection when it is turned toward her. If you persist in trying to study her, however, she first disintegrates, then dissolves into nothing at all.

E. B. White once said a similar thing about humor, which "can be dissected, as a frog, but the thing dies in the process and the innards are discouraging to any but the pure scientific mind." You can't get at romance, then, by good old Western reductionism.

Understand, I am not just talking about romance in the sense of love between two people. You can't really have a romance with someone else unless you are, first of all, a romantic yourself. Most people I know are not very romantic. They were once, or had the chance to be, but romance got lost along the way, drowned in the roar of our times, beat out by overly analytic teachers, drummed out by those who scoff at romantics as foolish and weak. In those people, romance looked around and said, "I'm not living here; too cold."

What do romantics look like? You can't really generalize. Besides, to make a list of characteristics would be to commit the sin of breaking romance down into small pieces, which I cautioned about before. The best way to tell a romantic is to just be around one. You'll know. There is a sense of passion about them, a sense of living just a bit too far out at the edge emotionally, sometimes; a caring for what seem to be dumb things—an old chair you sat in during your graduate student days and in the early times of your career, a knife that lies on the desk year after year, a simple wooden box. You can tell a romantic by the voice—it dances because the mind is dancing.

And I can tell you this for sure: All romantics like dogs and cats, and maybe some other creatures, preferably animals that come in off the road for a little sustenance and decide to stay around and participate in the craziness they sense in this place of food and laughter. Animals like romantics, for they know they will never be let down by them.

It's important to note here that you do not have to be a poet or a painter or a musician to be a romantic. In fact, I know quite a few folks in these areas of endeavor who are downright unromantic. On the other hand, Andrew Carnegie was a romantic. So was Joseph Smith when he led the Mormons westward. And I have seen more than one insurance salesman, in the bars where I have played, grin outwardly and inwardly when I launched into a song about the wind and the flowers and the highways that run forever.

Robert Pirsig puts it well, in his book *Zen and the Art of Motorcycle Maintenance*, when he says, "The Buddha ... resides quite as comfortably in the circuits of a digital computer or the gears of a cycle transmission as he does at the top of a mountain or in the petals of a flower. To think otherwise is to demean the Buddha—which is to demean oneself."

In a sense, romance is practical. It fuels your life

and propels your work with a sense of vision, hope, and caring. Because you are working for others, not just for yourself, your work takes on a certain quality that it will not otherwise have. I suppose you can say romance puts meat on the table, though, as I say that, I feel more than just a slight drain on my system as romance prepares to leave.

Let me turn now to the matter of getting and keeping romance. Romance is hard to get, hard to keep, and fairly easy to drive away. If you are really intent on getting rid of romance, though, here are a few brief suggestions:

Become obsessive about neatness, particularly in the way your desk looks.

Install expensive shag carpet in your house, so that when the dog throws up or one of your friends spills a beer, all hell breaks loose.

Don't listen to any good music. Ignore Bach, Mozart, Pete Seeger, and the Paul Winter Consort. Instead, listen only to top-40 radio. This is a first-rate approach to giving romance a shove out of your life, for she likes subtlety and low decibel counts.

Excessive focus on detail and procedure at the expense of vision, of dreams, of reflection, is another good way to get rid of romance. We in the academic world have mastered this approach.

Buy birthday cards, anniversary cards, and the like instead of making up your own. All of us are poets; some have just lost their voices for a while. As Ray Bradbury once said, about people in general, "And they were all, when their souls grew warm, poets."

Finally, the surest way to lose romance forever is to do things just for money, even though your cells tell you this is not what you should be doing.

Now, in no particular order, here are some suggestions for keeping romance around you (or getting her back if she has flown):

Read some poetry every day. For starters, try a little Yeats, then some Kipling (along with some of his stories). I know Kipling must be terribly out of fashion nowadays, but romantics never concern themselves with fashion anyhow.

Set a new schedule for yourself and do your reading then. Try this: Instead of flopping around in bed, get up early—maybe 4 A.M.—on a Sunday, in the winter, when a classic Iowa howler is blowing in from the Dakotas. This works pretty well. Besides, you have the secret pleasure of being reasonably sure you are the only one in the Western Hemisphere reading Kipling at that very moment.

Here's another idea. Sometime in your life, build your own house or at least the most intimate parts of it. Design it, too, with lots of thought. You will get endless pleasure and romance from walking through doorways and knowing you put the door there with your mind and your hands.

Collect little things, like the old knife on your desk or the small box you had for keepsakes when you were a child. At a time in my life when I was just overcome with administrative burdens, and my face showed it, one of my faculty gave me a small wooden flute along with a note that said, "Don't let your muse slip away." I keep the flute where I can see it.

Play a musical instrument. Something you can get out on those early mornings when reading is not the thing. Don't tell me you are not musical and, for heaven's sake, don't tell me you are tone deaf. I simply, if you'll pardon the expression, won't hear of it. If all else fails, or even if it doesn't, buy an Appalachian dulcimer. You can get warm, exotic sounds out of it right away without knowing anything formal about music at all. Try reading some ancient Chinese poetry while you strum the dulcimer. It works wonders.

Travel is good for romance. But don't just travel; *travel*. Here's what you need: notebooks, a small compass, a pocket atlas of the world, and a spyglass for looking out of airplane windows or across the rooftops of Paris or far down the country lanes in England. A word of warning is needed here: If you are traveling with your boss and he or she is not a romantic, be careful. You may not want to be seen with your compass and a spyglass on an airplane. If you are a true romantic, however, it won't matter much, because you will be good at what you do and your boss will just shake his or her head and mutter about what one has to put up with to get quality work these days.

Keep good journals of your life and travels. This is vitally important. I delight in reading and re-reading my adventures in the old markets of Saudia Arabia, where I bargained for gold and silver to bring home, and my wild ride through the streets of Riyadh late at night with a Bedouin cab driver who played Arabic music on a tape deck and tried to give me a short course in his language, while the best I could do was teach him to say "Kleenex" by pointing to a box of it on his dashboard.

I like knowing that I was in Richmond, Virginia, at 7:55 A.M. on June 7, 1981, or that I was in Paris in the snow in January 1982, or that I was once in Montego Bay, Jamaica, in the spring.

One of the most haunting entries in my journals reads, "12:24 P.M. Back in Iowa Georgia and Rachael are sleeping (3:24 A.M.), and I'm over Egypt." When I wrote that, I remember feeling very far away, in more ways than just miles, somehow.

My secretary leaves me alone when I fall behind in an especially unappealing piece of work, and a cold, gray, November rain is splattering against the third-floor windows of Seerley Hall. She knows I'm traveling. I stand, put my hands in my pockets, stare out those windows, and I'm comforted by the knowledge that somewhere the big planes are turning for Bombay or Bangkok, for Brisbane or Barcelona, and romance is skipping along their wings.

But romance is not just outward bound. She also rides your shoulder when you turn for home, with your notebooks full, your suitcase packed with dirty clothes, when it's only a few days before Christmas and London's Heathrow Airport is pandemonium, with all flights overbooked. But then you're on, in your seat, London falls behind, Ireland is below; you get out the notebook again, and you write, "God, all I want now is to see Georgia, Rachael, the pups, Roadcat, and eat a giant plate of Georgia's world-famous spaghetti."

Finally, you've got to work at remembering that romance is all around you. It's not somewhere else. Here are two examples.

I had to go to the Hawaiian island of Oahu a while back. Everyone told me, before I went, how crass and junky Oahu and, particularly, Honolulu have become. It certainly looks that way, at first glance. "But," I said to myself, "romance must still be here somewhere." At first I couldn't see her. My vision was blocked by Don Ho standing around drinking a piña colada. But something caught my eye—and there was romance, right behind him, jumping up and down and waving to me. So, I got up before dawn, went down to the beach, rolled up my jeans, waded in, and stood there in the pre-dawn grayness, playing my flute with the water washing around me and thinking about what this must have looked like when Captain Cook first came around Diamond Head, his sails flapping in the trade winds. There were a few other people on the beach, but they paid me no mind; they were there for the same reasons. When I finished, I heard the sound of applause from a long way off. I turned; it was romance. I caught a glimpse of her, just as the first ray of morning sunlight struck the barrier reef while she danced along it. And, my notebook says, "Soft winds blow easy, here in the night time, as Oahu lies bathing in the sweet scent of orchids. This skyplane will ride the west wind to morning and land in L.A. just after dawn."

The second example has to do with Iowa. Iowa is a very romantic, mystical place. I can't explain it, but it's here. Anybody can see the Rocky Mountains—they're obvious. It takes a little more perspective to see the beauty of Iowa or the romance in the long sweep of North Dakota prairie west of Larimore. Once when I was working in the woods south of Wadena, in northeast Iowa, it started to snow late in the day. I worked on. As I did, I began to feel a presence. What was it? The woods were filling up with snow. What was there? It took me a moment, but then I knew: It was Iowa. Iowa, like romance, doesn't come up and pirouette before you, saying, "Hey, look, I'm beautiful." She just lies there, on hot June days, like a woman in the sun, while romance splashes around where the Winnebago runs to kiss the Shell Rock, just two miles below the place of my growing.

Well, that's enough. You get the idea. All I have left for you is a test of sorts (you knew there would be a test, didn't you?). How are you going to know if you have lived the romantic life? Here's how. On your dying bed, after all the living and doing, you must run this poem by turn-of-the-century poet R. M. Rilke through your mind:

> *I live my life in growing orbits,*
> *which move out over the things of this world.*
> *Perhaps I never can achieve the last,*
> *but that will be my attempt.*
> *I am circling around God,*
> *around the ancient tower,*
> *and I have been circling for a thousand years.*
> *And I still do not know,*

if I am a Falcon,
or a storm,
or a great song.

When you have done that, on your dying bed, if you can smile and nod quietly to yourself, you will have succeeded, and romance will ride your shoulder as you turn for home.

Go well. Remember the flowers. Remember the wind. Thank you.

A Rite of Passage
in Three Cushions

I've always liked personal-sized heroes. In the early 1950s, when other boys were fawning over Duke Snider or Rocky Marciano, I was deifying Sammy Patterson in an unpretentious room on the main street of Rockford, Iowa.

I can still see him. Baggy shirt and pants. Flask protruding from his right hip pocket. He walked slowly and spoke quietly. But when he bent over the billiard table, his cue moved with the silent accuracy of an archer's

Originally published in *The Des Moines Register*, December 2, 1984.

arrow. His stroke was smooth and sure, and the result was never harsh, just the soft click of ivory against ivory, as the balls moved in complex patterns over the green cloth. He must have been about sixty then.

This was no fancy parlor where Sammy practiced his trade. No tuxedos, no leanings toward precious respectability with big prize money and women in evening gowns. Here, in Gerald Braga's "The Sportsman," pool was pool and billiards was billiards.

In case you have led a life more sheltered than I care to imagine, pool tables have pockets, billiard tables do not. At least this was true in the world in which I grew up. Billiards is played with three balls. Two white, one red. One of the white balls has a small spot on it to differentiate it from the other. One player shoots the "clear" and the other commands the "spot." The object is to make your cue ball hit each of the other two balls in one shot. A carom, in other words. Sound easy? It is not. Billiards is a game of physics, geometry, composition, skill, and treachery.

And Sammy was good, very good, at it. He covered three angles on each shot. Make the carom. Set yourself up for the next shot. Leave nothing for your opponent in case you miss. He taught me just about everything he knew, including how to hold ordinary pool players in infinite disdain, as I followed him around the table, night after night, dragging a cue as tall as I was.

I entered Sammy's world through a rite of passage. All cultures have these, and mine was no different. One Sunday morning my parents and I drove over from Rockford to have dinner with my grandparents in Charles

City. After we arrived and my mother had hurried off to the kitchen, my dad looked at me with a glint of wickedness in his eyes and said, "Let's go up to the Elks Club."

For an eleven-year-old boy, this was tantamount to being invited into manhood. It was the big leagues. Locked doors, a bar, silence on a Sunday morning, rumors of slot machines in the basement, and the smell of booze, smoke, and modest indiscretion left over from the previous night's party. It was a man's world. Women were invited for the parties sometimes; children were invited never, except for the annual Christmas bash, when the place, the language, and the behavior were sanitized.

My dad walked past the bar, flipped on the light over a pool table without breaking stride, and stood before the long racks of cues. Like a scholar gently perusing books in a sacred library, he ran his fingers lightly over the cues, pausing now and then to turn one and look at the number engraved on it indicating its weight.

He selected two, rolled them on the table to make sure they were straight, and casually slipped a few balls, including the cue ball, from the leather pockets. The training began. "Never, ever, shoot hard, except in special cases." "Here, spread the last three fingers of your left hand on the table, crook your first finger over to meet your thumb, and control the cue by running it through the circle made by your finger and thumb. Only amateurs put all five fingers down and run the cue over the place between the finger and the thumb." "Here's how English works." "Here are some tough shots and how to handle them."

55

It went on like that. For several weeks, each time we drove to Charles City on a Sunday morning, we shot pool. My dad was a fine player. I learned from watching him. Learned the language and the moves. Learned to take it seriously.

After the training, I was turned loose at Braga's place (we never called it "The Sportsman"). Braga and my dad were fishing buddies, so who knows what kind of pact was forged to assure my mother that, indeed, I would be all right there behind the steamed-over windows, lost in the thick smoke, and subject to the wild yelling and pointed oaths that came from the card room in the back, the room that had a sign saying "No Miners" tacked to its swinging-door entrance. (I remember pondering the fact that there was not a mine within 100 miles of Rockford.)

It was a dime a cue, loser pay, and it nearly always was crowded. My pool and fishing crony, Dennis Parker, and I headed for there every afternoon when we escaped from school. And, of course, weekends were best. On Fridays we raced to Braga's, put a nickel in the pinball machine, hoisted it up on our toes when Gerald wasn't looking, and ran up 200 free games, enough to keep us going for hours. One of us shot pool, one played pinball, and then we traded off.

I used to sit in school and dream of the beautiful patterns the pool balls made as they rolled, contemplating strategies for difficult shots. I kept shooting and got better. Pretty soon, I could spend all weekend in Braga's for an outlay of maybe forty cents, not counting the mustard-smeared hot dogs I ate from the machine that went round and round by the cash register. Sometimes Gerald hired me to rack balls on Saturday nights. I picked up a dollar for the evening doing that and actually showed a profit for my day.

I acquired my own cue for $5 from Kenny Govro. Kenny, it was said, had a bad heart and counted on his American Indian wife, Snow, to support him. He claimed he was giving up pool and billiards, in a fit of anger over losing one night, and sold me the cue.

It was a thing of beauty. Seventeen ounces of light-colored gleaming wood, cork grip, trimmed in ivory. An arrow for the wars that consumed me. It rested quietly in a special, locked rack fastened to a wall inside the card room, until I gently removed it each day and began to shoot pool ("miners" were allowed in the card room to get their private cues).

My mother was worried. Remember, this was only eighteen miles southeast of River City. She could spell trouble, she knew it started with *t*, and she knew what that fateful letter rhymed with. But she was over-matched. I shot pool out front, my dad was in the card room playing pinochle, and at least she knew where I was.

The only real concession she demanded, and she stood absolutely firm on this, was that I undress on the back porch and leave my "awful, smelly clothes out there." Those were her words. I thought I smelled just fine, anointed as I was with smoke, mustard stains, cue chalk, and the unmistakable musk of burgeoning skill.

At some point, I don't remember when, I was allowed to try the billiard table. This was another step in the rite of passage, as significant as learning to play pool. The billiard table was Gerald's glory. He kept its smooth, unmarked surface and lively cushions covered with light canvas when it was not in use. The balls were stored safely out of reach in a box behind the front counter. You had to have Gerald's permission to play on the billiard table. Perhaps twenty people held that permission at any time.

There is a beauty about billiards that's hard to explain if you never have played. It's like watching a ballet, or listening to Bach. It contains within it pure form, an aesthetic of motion, point and counterpoint, fugue-like movement, and the sense of a small universe into which one can plunge forever.

It was a different place from the cacophony of the pool tables only a few feet away. A place of silence, of concentration, of men who knew what they were doing. And Sammy Patterson ruled that world with a fearsome and undisputed grip.

The showdown was, I suppose, inevitable. The teacher, the student, the game. There are vectors at work out there that we do not understand, that bring us together in particular settings at chosen times, with the outcomes known only to those curious gods of chance and logic.

If there was a definable cause, though, it had to do with Kenny Govro. Kenny was regarded as the second-best billiards player in town, some distance behind Sammy. Shortly after his announced retirement from the game, he decided to renege on his promise and was casting around one night for someone to play. All he could find was the kid who had bought his cue. Oh well, a little practice to get the rust off. I slaughtered him. Sammy's teaching and the constant practice were working.

Kenny blamed it on the loss of his cue, re-entered retirement, and left Braga's cursing about cues and smart-aleck kids and life in general. My shellacking of Kenny may have convinced Sammy that it was about time to see what the kid could do.

It all came down on one of those hot, humid Iowa evenings in June, around 1953. I was in the general vicinity of fourteen by this time. Sammy and I never had really played a serious game. Instead, he would set up shots, show me how to attack them ("medium left English, off the left side of the red ball, hit the side cushion, then the end cushion, then the other side, and it'll head right for that old spot ball down in the corner"), and generally was trying to make a first-class billiards player out of the kid who followed him around.

I can't remember how the game got organized. There always was a certain mating dance that occurred when two good players were going to have at it. But, somehow, the little buttons on the wires overhead where the points were kept got shoved back, and the cues were chalked.

Word had flashed around in that mysterious small-town way that Sammy and I were going to play. Ordinarily, this would not have meant much, but the same communication system had already disseminated the news about my easy victory over Kenny, and a fair amount of interest was generated.

In fact, quite a lot of interest was generated. By

the time Sammy and I squared off, some twenty or thirty spectators had gathered. For a fourteen-year-old boy up against the Master, it was the Coliseum at noon, the sun and the sand, a matter of virility and honor lined out in some distant chant about young men and old lions.

We began. The match was to 500 points. I was on top of my game, running off strings of 20 or more points as my turn came. Sammy was not playing well. Perhaps it was the heat, perhaps it was because he had been conversing intently and at length with his flask while we warmed up. After a while, though, the magic welled up within him, and he began to make some long runs. It worried me. He was capable, I knew, of running off 75 points in one turn. I faltered, lost my confidence for a bit, recovered, and got back into it.

To this day, I can feel what it felt like then—the heat, the sweat, the smoke, the quiet murmuring of the men gathered around, and the old words of my father and Sammy flowing with clarity through my mind ("shoot easy," "high right English," "four cushions and get the red ball back up in the left corner," "if you are going to miss, don't leave him anything").

I began to see that I actually could win. I smelled and tasted the possibility. Teetering there on the brink of manhood, I got down hard and tight and mean. One or two long runs, and I had it. It was over. I couldn't believe it. Sammy looked tired, but I cared only that I had won.

I remember sprinting for home, bursting in and yelling, "I beat Sammy, I beat Sammy." My dad seemed surprised, went downtown to check out the facts, came home and didn't say much, except to congratulate me in a quiet way.

I didn't play much after that. Somehow, it wasn't the same. Mostly, I just strutted around with "Champ" written in invisible letters on my chest. I talked incessantly at home about the victory, and my father kept agreeing that, yes, it was quite a triumph.

A few weeks later, I strolled into Braga's. Dad was lounging against the counter talking with Gerald on a quiet Tuesday night. He grinned at me, "Son, want to play a little billiards?" Now, my dad was not a billiards player, just pool. Oh, he knew the rules and so forth, but he never played much. Cocky, I grinned back, "Sure."

Only Braga was there to see it. We chalked up, cleared the wires, and started. It was no contest.

My dad was a peculiar guy, good at anything requiring hand-eye coordination. He had worked something out with Gerald about practice time and had been bending over that green cloth for scores of hours, unbeknown to me. There was no letting up this time, as he sometimes did when he was beating me at pool in my learning days. He really went after it.

I was both rusty and rattled. He just kept grinning. Gerald watched, jingling coins in his change apron. I got mad and played worse. Dad played better. He scalded me. I refused his offer of a ride home and came sulking in a few hours later.

Other things took over my life. Basketball, falling in love, working. I never played much, if any, pool or billiards again. I came home from college once, went in to visit Gerald, walked around, and saw my old cue out in the public racks. It was battered from being slammed down on the pool tables when the "slop" players missed easy shots. I looked at it. It looked back dolefully, a mistress cast away for prettier things. Like the lovers that we were in an earlier time, we gazed softly at one another for a moment, sharing the memories rich and warm before I turned and walked away.

The lessons come slowly. Sammy died twenty years or so after that night of thunder and victory in Braga's place. Then Gerald went. Then my dad. The four of us were involved in a complicated dance, unchoreographed and intricate, unrehearsed and precise.

They taught me rhythms I have only recently begun to sense, melodies that escaped me until now—that Zen and precision are not at odds, that small universes exist if you acquire the discipline and skill to enter them, and that grace, passion, and an elegance of spirit are all that really matter, whether you're shooting billiards, making love, playing the guitar, winning, or losing.

You see, Gerald Braga didn't run a pool hall in a small Iowa town. He was the keeper of an academy. Sammy Patterson and my dad were among the faculty, and I, God love them all, had the good fortune to study there in the times when I was small, and tender, and wondering what it was like to be a man.

The Boy from
the Burma Hump

I n his apartment in Calcutta,
there was a grand piano. He wore khaki then, walked the
bazaars and tapped away at the piano or played lawn
tennis during his leaves from upcountry. After a week or
two, he was ready when the call came for the return to
Dinjan.

He carried only a small suitcase for the journey,
his "laundry" as he called it, and looked forward to getting back to the jungle and the mountains, away from the

Originally published in *The Des Moines Register*, April 8, 1990.

sterile and crumbling world of the British raj. His flight left Calcutta, climbing northeast over the Khasi Hills toward Assam, the secluded province that curls off main India and lies snuggled up on the left shoulder of Burma, just short of the Himalayan rise.

At Dinjan, he and the other pilots slept and took their meals in a large bungalow on the fringe of a tea plantation. Well before dawn, he was awakened by the hand of a servant boy. Now he stands drinking thick Indian tea on the veranda, looking out toward the jungle where leopards sometimes go.

An open four-wheel-drive command car arrives, and he rides through the heavy night toward an airfield five miles away. Time is important now, in this early morning of 1943. Since losing an airplane to Japanese fighters over the Ft. Hertz Valley, the pilots cross there only in darkness or bad weather when the fighters are grounded. He signs the cargo manifest, checks the weather report, and walks out to the plane.

Like delicate crystal, our liberties sometimes juggle in the hands of young men. Boys, really. Climbing to the top of the arch at the front of their lives, some of them flew into Asian darkness, across primitive spaces of the mind and the land, and came to terms with ancient fears the rest of us keep imperfectly at bay.

There was Steve Kusak. And poker-playing Roy Farrell from Texas. Saxophonist Al Mah, Einar "Micky" Mickelson, Jimmy Scoff, Casey Boyd, Hockswinder, Thorwaldson, Rosbert, Maupin, and the rest.

And there is Captain Charlie Uban. Khaki shorts, no shirt, leather boots, tan pilot's cap over wavy blond hair, gloves for tightening the throttle lock. He waits in the darkness of northeast India for his clearance from air traffic control in nearby Chabua. There are perhaps a dozen planes out there in the night, some of them flying with only 500 feet of vertical separation.

Captain Charlie Uban. Twenty-two years old, five feet nine inches, 141 pounds. Born in a room over the bank in Thompson, Iowa, when airplanes were still a curiosity and the long Atlantic haul was only a dream to Lindbergh.

Chabua gives him his slot, and he powers his C-47 down the blacktop through the jungle night, riding like the hood ornament on a diesel truck, with 5,000 pounds of small arms ammunition behind him in the cargo bay. He concentrates on the sound of the twin Pratt & Whitney engines working hard at 2,700 RPMs, ignoring the chatter in his earphones.

The plane, with its payload plus 800 gallons of gasoline, is two tons over its recommended gross flying weight of 24,000 pounds. Gently then, Charlie Uban eases back on the yoke, pulls the nose up, and climbs, not like an arrow, but rather in the way a great heron beats its way upward from a green backwater.

It gets dicey about here. If an engine fails, he does not yet have enough air speed for rudder control. And he's lost his runway, so there is no opportunity to chop the takeoff and get stopped. But he gains altitude, turns southeast from Dinjan, and flies toward that cordillera of the southern Himalayas called the Burma Hump.

His copilot and radio operator are both Chinese. In the next four hours, they will cross three of the great river valleys of the world: the Irrawaddy, the Salween, and the Mekong. In the place where India, Tibet, Burma, and Yunnan province of China all come together, the mountain ranges lining these rivers constitute the Hump.

This is the world of the China National Aviation Corporation (CNAC—pronounced "*see*-knack"). Jointly owned by China and Pan American Airways, CNAC flies as a private carrier under nominal military control of the U.S. Air Transport Command. In the flesh, CNAC is a strange collection of civilian pilots from the U.S., Australia, China, Great Britain, Canada, and Denmark.

They are soldiers of fortune, some of the best hired guns in the world at pushing early and elemental cargo planes where the planes don't want to go and where most pilots won't take them. As one observer put it: "All were motivated by a thirst for either money or adventure or both, and it was impossible to gain much of the first without acquiring a considerable amount of the latter."

Some were members of Claire Chennault's dashing American Volunteer Group—the Flying Tigers— mustered out of various branches of the U.S. military in 1941 to fly P-40 fighter planes with tiger teeth painted on the air coolers in defense of China. When the AVG was disbanded, sixteen of the remaining twenty-one Tigers decided to throw in with CNAC.

Dinjan is the penultimate stop, the last caravanserai, on the World War II lend-lease column stretching from the United States to Kunming, China. Along sea and air routes to Calcutta, and then by rail to Dinjan, moves virtually everything needed to keep China in the

66

war, including perfume and jewelry for Madame Chiang Kai-shek.

Japan controls the China coast and large slices of the interior. Until the spring of 1942, lend-lease supplies were shipped to Rangoon, freighted by rail up to Lashio, and moved from there by truck over the Burma Road to China.

Then Vinegar Joe Stilwell's armies, sabotaged by British disinterest in Burma and by the indecisive, factionalized, and corrupt government of Generalissimo Chiang Kai-shek, were driven north. With the Japanese owning Rangoon, the railhead at Lashio, and portions of the Road, China was closed to the outside by both land and water. So it fell to the pilots to ferry matériel from Dinjan to Kunming. To fly the Hump.

As he reaches higher altitudes, Charlie pulls on a shirt, chino pants, woolen coveralls, and a leather flight jacket. Going through 10,000 feet he switches over to oxygen. At 14,000 feet, he needs more power in the thin air and shifts the superchargers to high. Above the Hump now.

In summer, the monsoons force him to fly on instruments much of the time. With winter come southern winds reaching velocities of 100–150 miles per hour, and he crabs the plane thirty degrees off course just to counter the drift. Spring and fall bring unpredictable winds, frequent and violent thunderstorms, and severe icing conditions.

He will fly over long stretches where there is no radio contact with the ground, up there on his own,

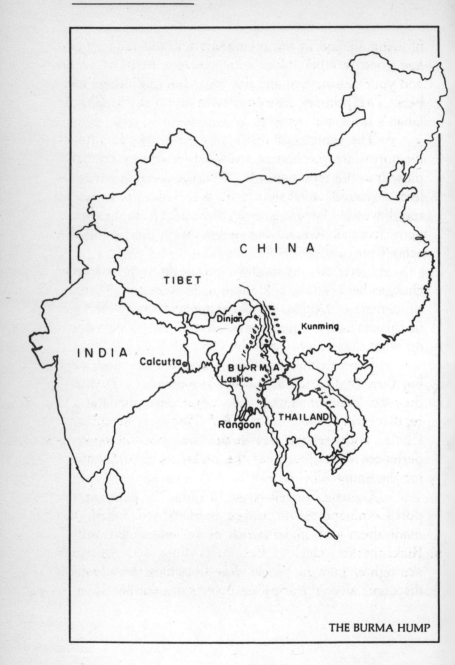

THE BURMA HUMP

blowing around in the mountains without radar. "You had good weather information on your point of origin and your destination, and that was about it," he remembers. The primary instruments in use will be Charlie Uban's skills and instincts.

The winds push unwary or confused pilots steadily north into the higher peaks where planes regularly plow into the mountainsides. And there are other problems. Ground radio signals used to locate runways in rough weather have a tendency to bounce from the mountains. Even skilled and alert pilots mistakenly follow the echoes into cliffs.

Electrical equipment deteriorates from rapid changes between the cold of high altitudes and the tropical climate of Dinjan. Parts are in short supply, navigational aids faulty or nonexistent. But maintenance wizards do what they can to keep the planes rolling.

Pilots fly themselves into fatigue, sometimes making two round trips across the Hump in one day. Still they go, their efficiency and competence shaming the regular army pilots in the Air Transport Command. CNAC, with creative, flexible management and more experienced pilots, becomes the measure of performance for the entire ATC.

General Stilwell wrote in 1943: "The Air Transport Command record to date is pretty sad. CNAC has made them look like a bunch of amateurs." Edward V. Rickenbacker, chief of Eastern Airlines and America's ace fighter pilot in World War I, studies the situation, discounts all of the army's problems with airports, parts, and maintenance, and simply concludes that CNAC has better pilots.

Charlie Uban is paid $800 a month for the first sixty hours of flying. He gets about $7 per hour, in Indian rupees, for the next ten hours. For anything over seventy hours, he is on "gold," $20 per hour in American money.

A 100-hour month earns him roughly $9,000 in 1987 terms. The rare melding of technical competence, practiced skill, good judgment, and courage always pays top dollar, anywhere. The CNAC pilots chronicle their exploits by making up song verses using the melody to the "Wabash Cannonball":

> *Oh the mountains they are rugged*
> *So the army boys all say.*
> *The army gets the medals,*
> *But see-knack gets the pay . . .*

Not everyone can do it. They arrive as experienced flyers and are trained for the Hump by riding as copilots, committing the terrain to memory, absorbing the mercurial techniques of high mountain flying, and practicing letdowns in bad weather. There is no time for coddling. Those who can't move into a captain's seat in a few months are discharged. Charlie Uban got his command in three weeks.

One veteran pilot makes a single round trip as copilot, is terrified, and asks to be sent home by boat. Others will hang on, but are so intimidated by the Hump that they develop neuroses about it and become ill. Or, bent by their fears, they make critical mistakes where there is room for none. The Hump, rising out there in the darkness and the rain, is malevolence crowned.

Was Charlie Uban afraid? He thinks about the question for a moment, a long moment, and grins, "I'd say respectful rather than fearful."

Fear and magic sometimes danced together in northern Burma. A Chinese pilot was flying a new plane from Dinjan to Kunming. Over the middle of the Hump, the temperature gauge for one of the engines began climbing. The instructions were clear: "Feather the engine at 265 centigrade." Panic arrived at 250 degrees.

With a full load, a C-47 will fly at only 6,500 feet on one engine. So the choices were three. Feather the engine and descend to an altitude that is not high enough to get through the mountains, let the temperature escalate and burn up the engine, or bail out in the high mountains. Three alternatives, each with the same outcome.

But the manual had been written by Western minds. Therefore, and not surprisingly, the range of options was unnecessarily constrained. As the gauge hit 265, the pilot broke the glass covering the gauge and simply twisted the dial backward to a reasonable level. Unable to get at the sender, he chose to throttle the messenger. There is some ancient rule at work here—if you can't repair the problem, at least you can improve your state of mind.

At Kunming, the gauge was diagnosed as faulty. The engine was just fine. Remember Kipling's famous epitaph? "Here lies a fool who tried to hustle the East." The C-47, like a lot of others, tried and failed.

If a crew goes down in the Hump region, no

71

search party is sent. The territory is wild and rugged, settled sparsely by aboriginal tribes or occupied by the Japanese. The snow accumulates in places to a depth of several hundred feet, and a crashed plane just disappears, absorbed by the snow.

The pilots suffer through it and gather strength from one another, talking quietly when a plane is overdue and cataloging the optimistic possibilities. After a few weeks, the missing pilot's clothing is parceled out among the others and his personal effects are sent home.

Charles L. Sharp, Jr., operations manager for CNAC, is a realist. Roosevelt demands that China be supplied. There is not enough time for proper training. The weather is wretched, equipment humbled by the task, and the planes, which are cargo versions of the venerable DC-3s, always fly above the standard gross weight.

So lives are going to be taken. Sharp accepts that. Still, he grieves for the pilots who vanish out there in the snow or thunder into foggy mountains during letdowns in China or blow up on the approach to Dinjan, and he worries about those who keep on flying.

Small samples from his logs in CNAC's war years intone a litany to risk and a chant of regret.

Aircraft No.	Captain	Date	Location	Crew
53	Fox	3/11/43	Hump	Lost
49	Welch	3/13/43	Hump	Lost
48	Anglin	8/11/43	Hump	Lost

72	Schroeder	10/13/43	Shot Down	Lost
59	Privensal	11/19/43	Kunming: let-down	Lost
63	Charville	11/19/43	Kunming; let-down	Lost

Between April 1942, when Hump operations started, and September 1945 at the end of the war, CNAC pilots will fly the Hump more than 20,000 times. They carry 50,000 tons of cargo into China and bring 25,000 tons back out. Twenty-five crews are lost. The consensus remains among those who understand flying that, given the conditions under which CNAC operated, the pilots were one of the most skilled groups ever assembled, the losses remarkably small.

Today Charlie Uban is freighting ammunition. Sometimes he carries fifty-five-gallon barrels of high-octane gasoline, a cargo he prefers not to haul. Or he might be loaded with aircraft parts or medical supplies or brass fittings. Occasionally he moves Chinese bank notes printed in San Francisco and being forwarded to deal with China's sprinting inflation.

On his way back from Kunming, he will be dragging tin or wood or hog bristles, or mercury or silk or refined tungsten ore. Now and then he has a cargo of Chinese soldiers going to India for training. They are cold and airsick for most of the trip.

As Stilwell begins his 1944 push back down into the jungles of Burma, Charlie will haul bagged rice that is booted out of the cargo doors at low altitudes to construction crews following the armies. The crews are building a new land route, the Ledo Road, from India across northern Burma to China.

Conditions are seldom good enough for daydreaming. Most of the time he concentrates on his gauges and listens to the engines, ". . . envisioning misadventures and figuring out what to do about them ahead of time."

But now and then in clear weather he thinks about other things. He thinks about his girl, Emma Jo, back in Iowa and calculates the days left before he gets his three-month leave in the States. And he remembers Charles Lindbergh's solo flight across the Atlantic in 1927. He was six years old at that time, but somehow understood the magnitude of Lindbergh's achievement even then. That's what brought him here.

His family moved to Waterloo, Iowa, where he grew up building model airplanes and reading magazine articles about the new world of flight. At fifteen, he bicycled out to the old Canfield Airport and used $2 from his *Des Moines Register* paper route to purchase his first airplane ride on a Ford Trimotor.

Bouncing around in a single-engine Taylorcraft, Charlie Uban learned to fly at Iowa State Teachers College in 1940 as part of the federally sponsored Civilian Pilot Training program. At Iowa State College in Ames he studied engineering and passed the secondary stage of the CPT program. He learned cross-country techniques at a school in Des Moines, taught flying for a while in Aberdeen, South Dakota, and was trained as a copilot for Northwest Airlines in Minneapolis, where he picked up his instrument skills.

When Pan Am wrangled a contract for supplying the Far East, he went to work for them and flew as a copilot in four-engine DC-4s and C-87s, hauling cargo and passengers down the Caribbean to Brazil and from there to Accra on the coast of West Africa. In Accra, the cargo was off-loaded onto smaller planes for the flight over the desert and across Asia to Calcutta.

In the summer of 1943 he was riding copilot alongside Captain Wesley Gray with a load earmarked for the Generalissimo himself. In Accra, they were ordered not to off-load, but rather to continue on across Africa and Asia to Dinjan, pick up a Hump pilot to guide them through the mountains, and take the cargo on into Chungking.

On the way, Charlie bumped into a few CNAC pilots and talked with one of them at length. Since Pan Am owned 20 percent of CNAC, he applied for a transfer, and by the fall of 1943 he was flying the Hump.

The C-47 settles down on the runway at Kunming. It's 9 A.M. Charlie will spend the day at a hostel near the airfield. He will nap, play cards, and talk with other pilots. In late afternoon, he takes off for the westward flight back to Dinjan. Tomorrow he will fly the same route once again. Often he will make one-and-a-half, or even two, round trips in a single day.

Charlie Uban made 524 flights over the Hump in two years and knows of only one CNAC pilot who claims more wartime crossings. After the war, CNAC moved its operations to Shanghai. Charlie went along, flying all over the orient—north to Muckden in China, west to Calcutta, and south to Manila.

75

Things got messy, though. Four planes crashed in one day in Shanghai due to weather and radio interference from commercial stations operating at illegally high power levels. The Chinese communists had begun firing on the CNAC planes, and there was dissension among the pilots over the way operations were being run.

Charlie had enough and came home to finish his mechanical engineering degree at Iowa State. He graduated in 1949 and entered the family oil business in Waterloo. In 1964, and again in 1968, he was elected to the Iowa legislature as a state representative.

The CNAC Alumni Association meetings are important to him. Friends come by. "I see Kusak and Norman there. It's an occasional refurbishing, a touching again . . . all the time, throughout the decades."

The old pilots talk about airplanes and mountains. Some flew for commercial airlines after the war or opened restaurants or farmed. Others, they say, smuggled gold through Asia and flew contraband in South America. There is a bond of forever among them. They bellied up against death, saw it all, and delivered the goods.

Any regrets about getting out of flying? Some. But Charlie Uban has looked backward, looked forward from there, and is comfortable with his choices. Yet he has a recurring dream in the nights of his life, even now. In the dream, he is flying low toward obstacles, trees and mountains and such, and there is never enough room to pass between them. He wonders about the dreams.

And *I* wonder what there is in the ordinary machinations of life to rival flying the Hump at twenty-two. Can the adrenaline ever flow that swift again? Can there ever be another sound as pure to the soul as the landing gear coming down at Kunming or a sight like that of Everest and Kanchenjunga to the northwest on a clear day as you come in to Dinjan?

Most of us think of life as a long upward sweep to some modest glory in our middle years. But if you have battled the great whale in your early times, what can ever compare? Maybe Hannibal or Lindbergh or the foot soldier at Normandy or even Orson Welles also suffered these proportions.

On the other hand, maybe none of this is important. Maybe it is enough to have done it and to live a life on the memories of having done it—of having swept upward from a thousand blacktop runways into the jungle nights on your way to China.

Others will do it again, but not in that place, in that way. The Hump, as a presence, has disappeared. It was a concoction of the times and the available technology. In a jet airplane, at 40,000 feet, the Hump no longer exists.

It's been forty-two years since Charlie Uban flew the Burma Hump. He talks about those times, late of an April afternoon, while Emma Jo makes supper noises in the kitchen. "I remember the time I realized I was doing an excellent job of flying this tough, tough route, and it just did wonders for my self-esteem." "If you're doing a good job, and somebody knows it and appreciates it, that's about as good as life gets."

His khaki uniform with a CNAC patch on the right shoulder drapes from the back of a chair. He wears a bush jacket from his India days and shuffles through

77

piles of flight maps and logbooks and picture albums on the table in front of him. As he warms to the memories, his voice alternates between the past and the present tense, and he speaks softly, more to himself than anyone else, running a finger gently along his recollections.

"Fall of '43. Two of 'em crash in Suifu, up the Yangtze River from Chungking. Robertson is still up there in the overcast, sees two puffs of smoke come up through the clouds, decides that's enough of that, and heads back to Dinjan." "A hundred and twenty-one hours this month." "Here! Hydraulic pump failure, good weather, short of personnel; flying the Hump solo, no copilot, no radio operator."

"Kunming, Dinjan, Kunming, Kunming. That means I had trouble leaving Kunming and had to come back in." "Next day, blower failure and had to return." "Next day, the 14th, rice dropping." "January 6, 1945, Russ Coldron disappears over the Hump." "January 7, 1945, my old friend Fuzzy Ball flew into Tali Mountain. . . ."

His voice trails off to a murmur as he reads. From his kitchen table in Iowa, Charlie Uban is reaching back four decades into the night and the wind and the deep snows of the southern Himalayas where some of his friends still lie.

I listen not so much to the words themselves, but rather to the sound of his memories. It's something like the drone of a C-47 cruising out there east of Dinjan, above the Burma Hump, in the days when it was pretty clear who was right and who was wrong. Over his shoulder I can see airplanes coming and going at the Waterloo Airport a mile away.

Just outside the window, wood ducks are circling among the trees by a pond, peering through the fog at the end of a rainy afternoon, looking for a place to land. Captain Charlie Uban watches the lead drake come in through the dusk on his final approach, sees him catch the headwind as he lets down through the haze, and nods his appreciation—from one old pilot to another.

Whether it's Dinjan or Calcutta, Kunming or Shanghai, or a small pond in Iowa, those who live on the wing understand one another. They have been taken aside by Iris, trained by scholars of the twilight. And, while the rest of us plead for guidance and struggle for the trace, old fliers have no need of that, for they know secret things and hear distant ragas that carry them along the great bend of the night toward home.

Ridin' Along in Safety with Kennedy and Kuralt

Indiana autumn. Blooming-ton, in 1967. The man comes through little swinging doors separating the dining room from the bar in the Holiday Inn. He smiles and asks, "Do you boys know the 'Wabash Cannonball'?" I do, but I haven't done it for a while. My partner, Wayne Schuman, riffles around on the five-string banjo for a moment, grins his funny little grin, nods to me. "Yeah, we can get through it," I say. The man and some friends are eating in the dining room and can hear the music just fine through the doorway. Back he goes to his table, carrying a napkin.

Originally published in *The Des Moines Register*, July 17, 1983.

Wayne and I crank it up—"From the green Atlantic Ocean to the wide Pacific shore . . ." I'm singing and playing the guitar, Wayne is flying along behind me, working out his instrumental break as he backs me up. "This train, she rolls through Memphis, Mattoon, and Mexico . . ." It's early. The bar is only a third full as we hit the chorus: "Listen to the jingle, the rumble, and the roar, as she glides along the woodlands, through the hills, and by the shore. Hear the mighty rush of engine, hear the lonesome hobo call. Ridin' along in safety on the Wabash Cannonball." We end and look at each other. Not bad for the first time through the tune together.

Back the man comes, through the swinging doors. Three others are with him. A round, familiar-looking fellow with friendly eyes asks if we'll play the song one more time. Playing the bars over the years has prepared me for things worse than singing a song twice in a row, so we do it.

After we finish, the round fellow holds out his hand. "I'm Charles Kuralt from CBS. We're doing a television piece on the death of the Wabash Cannonball, and we want you boys to play the music for it, right here in the bar." Confusion takes over. The motel manager is gone. The bartender, Cliff, is a suspicious sort, as bartenders are wont to be. This is his world, he's responsible for it. Finally, he agrees that Kuralt and his crew can do what they want, as long as nothing is damaged.

Confusion turns to chaos. Kuralt's old van is pulled up to the outside door of the bar. People are carrying lights, cameras, sound equipment. While this is going on, Kuralt interviews us. I'm writing my doctoral dissertation and playing here on weekends, trying to get my wife, baby daughter, and myself through the last year of an interminable number of years of school. Wayne is an undergraduate, playing mostly for fun.

People in the bar are agog, asking questions. We announce over the mike what is taking place. This leads to a crush at the pay phone in the lobby as they call friends ("Yes, yes, CBS Television is going to film the folksingers right here in the Holiday Inn bar."). Five minutes later cars start screeching into the motel parking lot. The friends are arriving. Chaos shifts to pandemonium. Cliff is mixing drinks at record pace, while the waitresses fight their way around equipment, over cords, and through people streaming in and about the bar.

Forty-five minutes go by; Kuralt's crew is ready. Sound test. Okay. The klieg lights come on; it looks like midday in what was a dark bar. The labels on the two big cameras in front of me say "CBS TELEVISION." "Jeez, this is for real," I think. The sound man lies on the floor at my feet, just out of view of the cameras, holding a large microphone that looks like it means business.

"All right," someone says, "start playing and don't stop until we tell you to." Sweaty hands. "Here's to Daddy Claxton, may his name forever stand . . ." Ten minutes later they flag down the Cannonball. Next, we do just the banjo part for six or seven minutes, Wayne's magical, double-jointed right hand waving like long grass in the summer wind as he picks.

It's over. "Yeah, thanks, we enjoyed it too." We take a long break. Cliff counts receipts and mumbles about "city folks." We stagger through the rest of the

83

night, continually rejecting requests to play the "Wabash Cannonball" one more time.

A few days later, TV on, and Cronkite smiles, "Here's a report from Charles Kuralt, who's on the road." There we are! We're on the screen for about a minute, hammering away, with some voice-over by Kuralt about the end of the Cannonball (he's riding on the last run). Kuralt interviews passengers and the conductor. At the end, an aerial view shows the train moving away, whistle blowing. They have synched the guitar and banjo with the clicking of the wheels. It's pretty touching. She fades into the distance, almost out of sight, and Kuralt says softly, "Tomorrow the Wabash Cannonball won't be a train at all, only a banjo tune."

Cronkite sighs, "That's the way it is . . ." My phone rings. It's an old friend from Connecticut, shouting. "I can't believe it! I just saw you on Walter Cronkite." We talk. I hang up, and the phone rings again. Everybody in the world watched Cronkite tonight. They run the tape the next day on a morning news show, then later on a program called "The Best of Charles Kuralt." We're famous, sort of.

A few months later the phone rings once again. A breathless voice asks if he's talking to the guy who did the Cannonball thing for Kuralt. Yes. He's from Robert Kennedy's campaign headquarters. The Senator saw the show and wants us to go with him on an old-fashioned whistle stop tour in Indiana, for which they'll take the Cannonball out of retirement. Will we go? Yes, but it will cost $200. He doesn't care what it costs. (I curse my inexperience.)

Small town in north Indiana. April 1968. On the train with journalists, TV crews, and lots of other people in nice suits just running around. We are instructed to report to the last car, the Kennedy car. Bobby, Ethel, kids, dog. They need publicity shots. Sixteen (I counted) cameras from around the world zoom in on the Senator, Wayne, and me—"Listen to the jingle, the rumble and the roar . . ."

First stop. Secret Service types lead us onto the back platform, guns visible when they turn just right. Bobby and Ethel follow them, then us. The Senator holds the mike for me. ". . . as she climbs along the woodlands, through the hills and by the shore." Thousands of people, screaming, holding up signs for and against the Kennedy effort, pushing to get close to the platform. Men with cameras on their shoulders are fighting the crowd and trying to get a foothold on the slippery rails.

We go on, from town to town. The scene repeats itself. Guns, crowds surging, Bobby talking in his persuasive way about problems and people. He holds the mike for me as we pull away. "Ridin' along in safety on the Wabash Cannonball."

Back in Iowa, I receive the check from Kennedy campaign headquarters the morning he is shot. Strange. Probabilities. I somberly walk to the bank and cash it. Strange.

Bobby Kennedy is dead, Charles Kuralt is still on the road, and Wayne Schuman doesn't play anymore. I get out the old Martin guitar, late in the day, and once in a while I quietly sing, "Listen to the jingle . . ." Once in a while.

Jump Shots

In a Dakota February, the
wind never rests. Neither do the basketball fans. Both are
howling as I bring the ball upcourt in the North Dakota
State University fieldhouse. Old patterns before me.
Stewart shouting instructions from the sideline. Holbrook
loping ahead and to the right. Spoden, our all-American
center, struggling for position in the lane. Head fake left,
and the man guarding me leans too far. Dribble right.
Double screen by Holbrook and McCool. Sweat and

Originally published in *The Des Moines Register*, July 6, 1986.

noise, smell of popcorn. See it in slow motion now. Behind the screen into the air, ball over my head, left hand cradling it, right hand pushing it, slow backward spin as it launches. Gentle arc . . .

The ball just clears the telephone wire and bounces off the rim of the basket as I land on hard-packed dirt in the silence of an Iowa summer evening. Miles from the wind, years before the Dakotas. Bored with school and small-town life at thirteen, I have decided to become a basketball player. Absurd. Five feet two inches tall, 110 pounds.

I am untroubled by the impossibility of it all. Day after day, night after night in the weak glow of the back porch light, the ball goes up. One hundred more shots, and I'll quit. Maybe 200. Can't stop until I have five straight from twenty feet.

Freshman year. I try out for the high school team, which is just not done by freshmen. Freshmen are supposed to play on the junior high team. That's understood. I take a pounding, mentally and physically, from the upperclassmen. Yet, into the evenings, wearing gloves in late autumn, I work jump shots around the telephone wire. Merlin, the school janitor, ignores the rules and lets me in the gym at 7 A.M. on Saturdays. I shoot baskets all day, with a short break for lunch.

The Big Day. Twelve will be selected to suit up for the games. I feel that I have a chance. I have hustled and listened and learned. But about twenty people are trying to make the team, a lot of them are seniors, and there is the whole question of whether a freshman even ought to be out there. At the end of practice, the coach has us informally shoot baskets while he walks the gym with a list. Studying it, he begins to call out names, slowly, one every minute or so: "Mehmen" ... "Clark" ... "Lossee" ...

Eleven names have been called; eleven have gone to the locker room to select their uniforms. I can hardly make my shot go up, or dribble, or even think. The coach paces the gym, looks at his list. Three, four minutes go by. He turns: "Waller."

There is silence; I remember it. A freshman? Wait a minute! I trot to the locker room with a feeling that comes only a few times in a life. The locker room is silent, too. I am not welcome, for all those complex reasons having to do with tradition and adolescence and the 1950s' definition of masculinity. Even Clark, the thoughtful one, shakes his head.

The remaining uniform is the largest of the entire lot. The pants can be cinched in to stay up, but the shirt is so big that the armholes extend down into the pants when it is tucked in. If it weren't so funny, it would be grotesque. But nobody is laughing.

Running through the darkness of a 1953 November evening, squeezing the neatly folded purple and white jersey, I explode through the back porch and into the kitchen. My parents are stunned. They have humored me through all of this, knowing how sensitive I am about my size. But they never expected success.

My dad is concerned for my safety. "Those big guys will make mincemeat out of you." My mother is worried about my schoolwork. But I care only about getting that damn suit to fit. Mother takes enormous tucks in the shoulder straps until the armholes assume somewhat normal proportions. The armor fits. The warrior is ready.

Our yellow bus rolls through a midwestern winter with Hank at the wheel. St. Ansgar, Greene, Nora Springs, Riceville, Manly, and on and on, through the Corn Bowl Conference. I ride alone in my jeans, green checkered shirt, and engineer boots, ostracized. A good friend of the seniors has been left home because of me. On the bench, I watch closely. The season is not going well.

Gradually, and mostly out of desperation, the coach looks down the bench and says, "Waller, get up here." Occasionally there is a chance for the long jump shot that arcs into the bright lights of a dozen high school gyms, slicing the net on its way through the basket. The other players are a little kinder to me. By the final game of the season, I am there. I start. We pound up and down the floor at Nashua, winning. I score 12 points. Merlin lets me in the gym the next morning at seven, grinning, with news of the game from the café. "Twelve points, huh?"

More time on the dirt in the summer. "Ya, I'll be in for supper in a minute." Can't quit until I hit ten in a row from twenty feet.

Sophomore year. It's a winning season. I start every game. We upset Rudd, a powerhouse, in the county tournament, and the world is colored good. Merlin shows up smiling when I rattle the gym doors on Saturday mornings.

The back-porch light burns late in warm weather.

Can't quit until I hit fifteen in a row from twenty feet. My dad has taken an interest in the whole affair by this time and has the telephone wire moved out of the way. Mother worries about my schoolwork and cooks as if I am a one-man harvest gang. I am five feet ten without warning.

Junior year, new coach. Paul Filter has a low tolerance for dolts. He smiles a lot, but his starched white shirts and neatly pressed suits give him away. This is a serious guy. Serious about teaching history, serious about getting young boys in short pants ready for basketball and for life beyond, a life I cannot conceive of.

We have lost most of our starters and struggle through a break-even year, improving as we go, while Filter lovingly calls us "clowns." But the jump shot is there, game after game, in the hot gyms. On some nights twenty of them go in from far outside.

Paul Filter begins to see what I am up to and designs a training program for me in the off-season. Roadwork and push-ups (no high school weight-training programs around in those days). I do 140 push-ups at one time and grow to six feet. It's getting serious.

Something, though, is at work that I do not completely understand. This is more than a game. I think deeply about the art and physics of the jump shot and ponder these while I practice. The search for perfection, the ballet-like movement, soft release, gentle arc, the reward.

My last year rolls up, and I ride the momentum of years of steady practice. The jump shot floats through the Iowa winter nights. The points mount up game by game—39, 38, 45, 34. I play with two people guarding me in most games, three one time. But the roadwork, the push-ups, and, of course, the jump shot are there with enormous force. The other teams are not prepared for someone training at a near-professional level. Mo Parcher and Bill Mitchell grab rebounds, Tommy Ervin sets screens for me, and we win our first twenty-three games.

Filter keeps teaching. He has long conversations with me about getting athletics into perspective. He is aware that I will have offers to play college basketball, and he is trying hard to get me ready for something more. I sulk when he takes me out of the St. Ansgar game at the end of the third quarter. I have 39 points and have just hit nine out of ten shots in that quarter as we bury the Saints. I want to stay in and break my own single-game scoring record. Filter moves me far down the bench and refuses to even look at me as he coaches nervous and eager sophomores. The next morning he talks long and hard to me about sportsmanship, perspective, and life.

It ends against Greene in the tournaments. We have beaten them twice before, but they dig in and go at us. My long jumper goes in and out with no time left. Over.

A few days later, a letter comes from Bucky O'Connor, coach at the University of Iowa. Can I come to the campus for a visit and see the Fabulous Five play?

My dad and I spend the day with Bucky, go to a game, and exist in the realms of the privileged. Bucky will recruit four players this year, and he wants me to be one of them. My dad soars. He has spent a lifetime of evenings listening to the Iowa ball games.

We sit at the kitchen table and fill in the scholarship forms. Dad and I laugh and talk about jump shots in the Iowa fieldhouse. Mother says only one thing: "I think this boy should go to college to study something, not to play basketball." What? We verbally abuse her, and she stops talking nonsense.

My first jump shot at Iowa is a memorable one. Early-season scrimmage, and I confidently move downcourt. All the old rhythms are in place. I stop, go into the air, perfect timing, great release, and the tallest person I have ever seen knocks the ball back over my head to the other end of the court. Some adjustments will be necessary.

I don't know much about playing defense or even team basketball. The kids from the cement playgrounds of Chicago and Louisville do. "Okay, Waller, you don't get to play on offense anymore until we say so. Whenever the ball changes hands, you go over to the defensive side."

The jump shot is silenced for a while. Nonetheless, the coach says I am the greatest natural shooter he has ever seen. I grin at the word "natural" as I think of those seven o'clock mornings in the gym. Somewhere, Merlin the janitor also grins.

There is, however, something more going on in my eighteen-year-old head. The feelings are not clear, but they have to do with the words of Paul Filter and my mother. I like Tom Ryan, my humanities teacher, and also a strange little man who teaches literature. I do poorly in school, though, and blame it on basketball. My freshman year drifts by. Everybody exclaims about the jump shot while waiting for me to develop other areas of the game. And Bucky O'Connor is killed in an auto accident.

A ruptured appendix in the summer, a broken finger, and a nasty knee injury early in the fall get me off to a slow start the next year. I am now haunted by these other feelings. I am close to falling in love with a young woman whom I will marry eventually. And the old curiosities from my boyhood, when I read most of the books in the Rockford library, are surfacing.

Other things bother me, too. Somehow a boy's game has been turned into something else. Grown-ups outside the university actually care about our sprained ankles and the quality of our man-to-man defense. I cannot attach the level of importance to winning that seems to be required. Practice and films and practice and films. Locker-room talk in which women fare poorly leaves me cold. The special study sessions for athletes where amazingly accurate information about upcoming examinations is handed out are repugnant. On principle, I refuse to attend these sessions and am laughed at for it. There is something wrong, deadly wrong, and I know it.

I drop out of school. My father is disappointed and hurt in ways he cannot even express. A few months of menial work, and Iowa State Teachers College takes me in. No scholarship, no financial aid. My parents send money, and I work at a local bank. Good basketball in a lower key.

Norm Stewart comes to coach. He teaches me more about defense in three weeks than I have learned in a lifetime. Mostly, aside from keeping your rear end down and staying on the balls of your feet, he teaches me that defense is pride and gives me tough assignments in the games. I like that. It fits the way I am starting to think about the world.

The purple and gold bus rolls through the midwestern winters with Jack at the wheel. I stand up front in the door well and gather images for the songs and essays to come. The jump shot is still there. But things are different now. I am studying literature, playing the guitar, spending Saturday mornings reading Clarence Darrow's great closing arguments to his juries, and wallowing in all the things that college and life have to offer.

I am so deeply in love with a woman and with music that basketball becomes something I do because people expect me to do it. Seldom do I reach the levels I know I can touch with the jump shot. Oh, there are nights, in Brookings, South Dakota, and Lincoln, Nebraska, when twenty-five feet looks like a lay-up, the way it used to look in Riceville and Manly, and the baskets are there for the taking. Mostly, though, the old magic is gone.

Still, my dad drives down from Rockford on below-zero nights to watch what is left of it. He sits along the west sideline in the old teachers college gym, and, moving downcourt, I can pick his voice out of 4,000 others, "Go get 'em, Bobby." He was there with the same words, years ago, on winter nights in all the Corn Bowl Conference towns.

He calls on a March morning to say that I have made the All-North Central Conference first team. He heard it on the radio, he is pleased, and I am pleased for him. I ignore my remaining eligibility, take some extra courses, and graduate.

There is one final moment, though. The University of Iowa seniors barnstorm after their season is over. Another player and I team up with a group of high school coaches and play them at the Manchester, Iowa, gym for a benefit. It's a good game. We are in it until the last few minutes when our big center fouls out, and I am forced to guard Don Nelson, later of the Boston Celtics. And, for one more night, the jump shot is there, just as it once was. Twelve of them go down from deep on the outside.

The jump shot, with some 2,500 points scribbled on it, has lain unused for over twenty years. It rests in a closet somewhere, with my old schoolbooks and Flexible Flyer sled. I got it out once to show my daughter, who asked about it. It took a few minutes to shine it up, and she watched it flash for a little while in the late-afternoon light of a neighbor's back yard. I put it away again. It was a boy's tool for a boy's game, for growing up and showing your stuff. Merlin knew that.

More than anything, though, and I understand it clearly now, the jump shot was a matter of aesthetics, an art form for a small-town kid—the ballet-like movement, the easy release, the gentle arc over a telephone wire through the summer nights of Iowa, while my mother and father peered out the back-porch screen door and looked at each other softly.

The Turning of Fifty

In my late forties, I came quartering down the years and forgot how old I was. When asked to give my age, I would run a quick cipher: "Let's see (mumble, move lips slightly) ... born in ... present year ... subtract ..." Was this a simple inattentiveness caused by the distractions of a busy life, I wondered? Or maybe, I wondered again, if some winsome sleight-of-hand by the mind itself was at work, the balming of harsh reality by a man growing older.

Originally published in *The Des Moines Register*, December 3, 1989.

In any case, others noticed it first. My turning fifty, that is. A few months before my birthday, people started speaking to me in peculiar tongues, saying things such as "Hey, hey, Bob-O, the BIG ONE's coming! How are you going to celebrate it?" "I'm too busy to have a birthday," I countered, shuffling away from the subject.

That was not good enough. Indeed, I was told, this is a seminal occasion and deep, indelible markings should be tooled upon the hours of August 1. So, when pressed, I would claim the day to be mine alone and declared I would spend it sloshing around in some quiet swamp with my cameras.

But I dawdled, made no plans, and others kindly took over. My friend Scott organized a small birthday party held two days before the actual date. Old friends were generous enough to attend, I sat in a lawn chair with red balloons tied to the back of it, and Scott took a class picture. That was as wild as it got. We had a genuinely good time, in a quiet way, and the affair fit my approach to things. Well, the balloons seemed a little out of character for me, but I thought afterward that everyone ought to spend at least one day a year sitting in a chair with balloons tied to the back of it.

I drove the sixty miles up to Rockford the evening before my birthday and took my mother out for dinner. Lifting my glass as she lifted hers, I grinned, "Thanks for getting me here." She smiled back, said she was proud of me, and told me again how the delivery took place in the middle of an Iowa thunderstorm and how the hospital lights failed just before I was born. I leave the significance of those latter two events open to various interpretations.

On the day itself, I put aside my low-fat, semiveg-etarian tendencies and ate two Maid-Rites. That was rather like an act of homage to my youth. For it was in Roger Dixon's Charles City Maid-Rite where I first lunched as a young boy, and I have retained a nearly religious zeal for the loose-meat sandwiches since then. As part of this, trips to Des Moines often are scheduled in such a way that a stop at Taylor's Maid-Rite in Mar-shalltown is not only possible, but inevitable.

There are, you see, few rituals more sublime than slowly spinning back and forth on a counter stool and watching sandwich makings being scooped from the steam table of a true Maid-Rite café. Truth in this case flows from a purity of undiluted purpose, a place where nothing other than Maid-Rites are served, except for the essential milk shake and graham cracker pie.

After the Maid-Rites, I took a nap, did my three miles on the road, read for several hours, and watched a movie. No "Over-the-Hill-Gang" T-shirts were pur-chased, no champagne was chilled, and bad jokes about getting older were avoided entirely. My wife wrote me a lovely note that said, "I'm short on words, but long on love," which I thought, apart from the sentiment, was a model of good writing and deserved a steel guitar lick underneath it. She also gave me a small crystal embedded in silver made by a local craftsman, and upon the silver were etched a fish and a falcon to represent my love of things wild and free. That was it, and it was just fine.

Still, the gentle lash of my friends and relations about the day's significance had its effect. In the midst of my reading that afternoon, I began to drift, thinking about time and the curious spiral dance of which I am a part. If I am just one of a long file of travelers, how about the rest? What were they doing on some other August 1?

Galileo, for example, in 1633. In April of that year, the Church had forced him, under threat of torture, to recant the conclusions reached in his *Dialogue Concerning the Two Chief World Systems* that Ptolemy had been wrong and Copernicus had been right: earth was not the center of all things heavenly. So I imagined Galileo Galilei in Florence, afraid, angry, and alone on a warm August day.

How did a shepherd ranging over the hills of Sumer, 2,000 years before Galileo, feel on this day? Did the flutter of light and shadow cause him to stop and think of a woman in a nearby town or how life is passing strange? Was the Rev. Thomas Bayes working on his famous probability theorem on the first of August in 1760? The beauty of his proof, which is taken by some as the beginning of modern statistics, consistently has escaped my students.

And Socrates. Where was he on a fine August evening? Making his way home with other guests from a night at Xenophon's, I suppose. The music was fading, but there was yet enough wine in the blood to stir their tongues as they moved through the quiet streets of Athens, the conversation still lively, still centered around matters at the heart of things.

Was Alexander out on the desert with his armies? Where was Geronimo a hundred years ago? And how did the infantryman walking along the French hedgerows in 1944 feel? On some August 1st was Charlie Parker practicing scales in E-flat major and Gertrude Stein holding court in Paris and Dali twirling his moustache? Was Swinburne writing "The world is not sweet in the end" on my birthday somewhere in the cool of England, while a black woman stared through a haze of Alabama heat at distant rain clouds?

Swinging around in my chair, I looked at what surrounded me and imagined a future archaeologist, perhaps some alien blob of magenta protoplasm, carefully brushing away the crust of five thousand years and making notes on what it found. "Computer keyboard—primitive method of data entry." "Guitar—well-preserved example of mid-twentieth-century instrument building." "Stapler—used for fastening papers together prior to the invention of laser bonding." "Camera—one of the last models predating portable, digital imaging."

Next, I reviewed my list of ways I do not want to die. For example, I have noted "In a hospital." And, "Tail-ended by a '74 Cadillac in front of K Mart while a blue-light special on men's underwear is commencing." Then I turned to the acceptable list. "Falling off a cliff in northern Iowa on a foggy morning while adjusting my tripod." Or, "A spear in the chest on the African veldt" (first preference).

I also remembered that, following his orders, the bones of Genghis Khan were carried about by his armies in the field after his death, as a kind of memorial. That's what morticians like to call "pre-need planning." Personally, I've always thought that Khan pushed things a bit, overstayed his welcome, as it were.

That was all good fun, but it took me no closer to anything fundamental than where I had been at the beginning. So I dug in a bit, started things running back and forth across the corpus callosum, and got down to basics, while the overhead fan turned slowly. "All right," I said to myself, "I'm gibbous, more than half-rounded, a long run from the chrisom and the breast. So what can be made of that? What do I know and feel here on a summer afternoon with a half-century stretching out in back of me?"

Ontologists searching for the meaning of existence generally leave me behind in their quest, at least in their writings. I suppose, as with other such matters, it would have helped to have been there, at the Café Flore with Sartre, de Beauvoir, and the rest when they gathered to deal with the foundations of being.

For me, I'm content with Waller's Second Conjecture: Existence takes on meaning only when you give it meaning by making it meaningful. And how do you make it meaningful? By listening to those almost-secret voices within you that, at certain critical times, whisper, "This is me."

In those moments, it's important to consciously note what you're doing and to do more of it, a lifetime of it, in fact. I think this is what Joseph Campbell means when he speaks of "following your bliss." In case this seems a little too narcissistic, a little too thin and self-focused, I also believe that the meaningful life must include a concern for things beyond yourself, including our animal friends, rivers, trees, and other humans.

For twenty years I have had the following verse by Bengali poet Rabindranath Tagore hanging above my desk:

The song that I came to sing remains unsung to this
  day.
I have spent my days in stringing and in unstringing
  my instrument.
The time has not come true, the words have not been
  rightly set;
Only there is the agony of wishing in my heart.

Those words have haunted me for two decades. And, as I move around, I think they apply to a fair number of people I meet. I now keep Tagore pasted above me more out of tradition than necessity. Somewhere, around forty, I began, though somewhat imperfectly, to get the instrument tuned, the words in order, and the melodies flowing. Ice skaters are required to learn school figures, basic stuff. Living is a little like that. You have to get the school figures down, get 'em cold, so you can execute them subconsciously.

When that happens, when the words began to flow and the melodies take shape, the search for meaning does not end, but life starts to become meaningful even as you seek to make it more that way. Others apparently get there earlier than I did. Many never do, and that is the great tragedy of our times and the failure of our civilization, for neither our religions nor our schools nor our informal social structures provide us with the tools to search, diligently, for meaning in this present life.

How do you know when you're getting there? Well, things feel right; there is a sense of unification, as if you are becoming a tapestry rather than a conglomeration of tangled threads, and you are doing the weaving yourself, almost effortlessly. Personally, I think the pursuit of trivia and rapacious, material acquisition so honored by this society thwart the search and inhibit the weaving, and that the arts are the prime vehicle for clarifying and accelerating the search. But that's another story for another time.

At some point, you have to deal with a hard and essential fact: you discover that the things you're good at and the things you love are not necessarily the same. Whatever wisdom I have, I tend to get much of it from strange places. One of them was an obscure film, *The Gig*, about musicians. A first-class professional is talking to a man who wants nothing more than to be a professional, but obviously cannot cut it. The pro is tired of the amateur's whining and obsequious pleas to join a band and says: "Music is not like religion; devotion is not enough." There it is. It's a good thing to know.

There's also the problem of doing away with the clutter. Like good composition of any kind, coming to grips with life requires a certain elegance of lifestyle, not in the sense of being fancy, but rather a consideration of what can be discarded in favor of simplicity. I propose there is an insidious plot to steal our time in the world we have created, and it's important to get rid of as many encumbrances as possible, including lawn care and excessive housekeeping. The sign my wife posted a long time ago says it rather nicely: "Today I Cherish, Tomorrow I Dust."

Even being a little antisocial helps. A friend of mine is fond of quoting something I said a few years back about my reluctance to attend events of borderline value:

"You have fewer people at your funeral, but you get more reading time." There are krakens out there gobbling your life, and it's crucial that they be spotted and nullified.

Then there are the quantity people who want you to try and live forever. You've got to watch them, too. I'm not talking here about commonsense matters of diet and personal habits. I'm talking about those who resent flyers and do all they can to ground them. They're everywhere with cautious, chirping advice: "Keep your hands in the boat," "Hang on to the latchkey," "Stay away from the road." Some people see dragons all about them. Avoid those people and fight the dragons when they come along.

When you feel yourself starting to become whole, it's all right to accept positions of power, but not before then. The overriding problem with our country, and our world in general, is that we are, in large part, managed by incompetents. Most of these are men who have spent their lives seeking power rather than themselves.

Consequently, we are confronted with the grotesque spectacle of working for childish figures—half-baked little generals with overblown egos and no more understanding of the search for meaning than some primitive, base organism spending its time feeding on the lives and feelings of others, guzzling them up like strained peaches, cackling to themselves as they play shell games with other people's destinies.

Moreover, somewhere along the way, I think it's crucial to deal with the damnable issue of mortality. There is, of course, the inevitability of it all—the end of life. As children, we are brought slowly to this understanding through events rather than introspection. A grandfather dies when you're eleven. It seems incomprehensible, at first.

But at the funeral parlor there are lowered voices and solemnity. The old man who was, more than anything, your friend lies there quietly. And it comes to you, maybe for the first time, that all of this is not unceasing. The first sense of loss is that of ice cream on Sunday mornings and the wonderful, atrocious lies with which he embellished the stories of his cowboy days. The second is more haunting: We are not everlasting.

So you begin to understand mortality, dimly though, and with a vague assuredness that it applies to others, but not to you. Around twenty-two, however, I endured what I call my "mortality crisis." For six months, almost involuntarily, I lay in bed at night examining the edges of my physiology, seeking peace with the tenuousness of it all. I lay there in the darkness, thinking and sweating, terrified at the prospect of my own death. That period was excruciating but healthy, I believe, for I determined that time and I should be wary allies, not opponents.

Then life gets busy, fears recede in the tumble of daily life. And nature helps in this. An inherent kindness exists in the process of aging. Except for the unforeseen miseries of homicide or wars or sudden catastrophic illness, we are allowed to move along gradually. Imagine, for a moment, that we looked and felt exactly the same at fifty as we did at twenty. But, then, on our fiftieth birthday, suppose we changed suddenly to the physical condition and appearance of, say, a ninety-year-old. That wouldn't work, psychologically. We graciously are given time to adjust. (Incidentally, I'm not denigrating the appearance of older people; I'm merely talking about change.)

In my bathroom mirror at home it works just this way. I see myself every morning. The changes are unnoticeable from day to day. But there are other reflections.

For the last ten years I have taught in an executive development program at the University of Richmond. I always visit there in June and am lodged in undergraduate student housing along with participants in the program. Such quarters are standardized, obviously, so even though I may shift from room to room over the years, the uniformity of the place provides the illusion that I am staying in the identical room each year.

This provides a benchmark of sorts. On each visit, scraping the shaving cream away, I have a chance to examine what twelve months have done to me. There is, I admit, a certain trauma connected with this annual experience. Yet, perversely, I also look forward to it as a kind of gruff and unforgiving timepiece, measuring my progress, telling the truth, refusing to lie.

And every June I am given over to marveling at the human capacity for handling the certainty of our own deaths, for writing our own obituaries even as we live. That we can comprehend our own demise and that we do not constantly whirl about in rabid frenzy at the thought of it is part of our magic, a built-in mechanism for sanity of the most powerful kind.

But the borders are there. They are stern and

ineluctable, and I see them approaching. Clearly I see them, on summer mornings, as I stare at myself in the mirrors of Richmond.

Yet, there are voices that speak to me along the rivers, along the way. With scolding words, they counter the momentary sag born of distant mirrors and honest appraisal: "Saddle up, caballero, and stop sniffling." They are right, of course. When Odysseus cried, "There is nothing worse for men than wandering," he was correct in the metaphor but wrong in the physical reality. There are Yaqui drums in high plains arroyos and ship engines north of Cairo I have not yet heard. There are beaches where you can still run naked at dawn and visions within a yard of my house that I have not yet seen through the lens of my Nikon.

I missed the last packet boat down the Missouri. It left from the Fort Lewis, Montana, levee in 1890. How I wish I had been on it, coming by places with names such as Malta Bend, just to have gathered in the sense of history and change that must have been stacked along the decks. But there are other boats. Some are Arab dhows with saffron-colored sails. They move through the waters of Ocean India, and I aim to sail upon such a boat along the Somali Current.

The voices of the river remind me that neither chemists nor alchemists can save me. And they tell me it's all right to remember, in Kipling's words, "That night we stormed Valhalla, a million years ago," that it's allowable to sing sweet lamentations for the death of blue autumns, but not to dwell upon those things entirely. For in the pleasant sorrow that comes from remembrance, time shifts in character. No longer an ally then, but a legendary bandit who'll steal your woman and take your passion and ride the evening train.

So the voices settle me. And I remember most of what I know that is good and true and lasting has come not from scholars but from minstrels and gypsies, from magicians and magic, from jugglers swallowing fire. It has come from small bands of travelers who followed the rivers and told me old stories and chanted old warnings of young women dancing through late afternoons and into the firelight, leaving only a footprint for the morning that follows.

Listening closely, then, I have learned that languor is not the price of serenity. I know there is more ahead of me than discounted airline tickets and shuffle-board, or a condo on the edge of a Scottsdale golf course. And, if it's all right with everyone else, I think I'll skip the midlife passage involving gold chains and Porsches and suntans.

Instead, I'm lacing up my twelve-year-old Red Wings, loading the cameras, putting new strings on the 1957 Martin flattop, getting ready to go where egrets fly. Like an old rider of the surf, I can already see the next wave coming. It looks fine and fair. It looks worth the effort.

I Am Orange Band

The thought is a haunting one. It comes to me at odd times, unpredictable moments. I might be playing my guitar or reading or just driving along in the car. And suddenly I'm thinking about a fellow named Orange Band. I never met him, and I never will.

His name resulted from a small strip of plastic around his leg. I used to think he deserved a better handle. In Latin he was *Ammodramus nigrescens*, but that seemed too coldly scientific and species-like, in the same way I

Originally published in *The Des Moines Register*, July 31, 1988.

111

am *Homo sapiens*. What was needed, I thought, was a name that captured in a word or two his unique place in the scheme of things. Something that identified him as being the very last of his kind, that succinctly conveyed the isolation of his existence. A name that somehow reflected the infinite loneliness that must accompany a state of undiluted unity. For he was perfectly and unalterably alone.

But, in the end, I decided that Orange Band was a good name for him. He was plain, and he was gritty, and it suited him well. Besides, the simplicity of such a name is more than fitting if you are the only remaining dusky seaside sparrow and there is no one left to call it out. If I were the last of *Homo sapiens*, I think I would take such a name. And I would sit with my back against a granite ledge, near a river in a distant twilight colored blue, and say, "I am Orange Band," listening to the words come back to me through the trees and along the grass.

How do we measure loneliness? If the counting bears any relationship to the number of your species still around, then Orange Band was lonely. It had not always been so. The duskies were common once in the marshes of Merritt Island, Florida. They were six inches long, blackish above with a yellow patch near the eye, streaked in black and white lower down, and sang a buzzy song resembling that of a red-winged blackbird.

That was before we slowly pitched our faces skyward and murmured, "Space." Along with the mathematics of flight and the hardware to take us there, we had to deal with the nasty problem of mosquitoes that plagued the Kennedy Space Center. For reasons known only to people who conjure up such things, flooding the Merritt Island marshlands nearby seemed to be the answer to the mosquito problem. The water rose and took with it the nests of the dusky seaside sparrows.

There was one other place, just one, where the duskies lived. Propelled by conservationist pressures, the federal government lurched into action and spent something over $2 million to purchase 6,250 acres along the St. John's River. There were two thousand of the little songbirds living there. Ah, but highways came. Always the highways come. They come to bring more people who will need more highways that will bring more people who will need more highways. The marshes were drained for road construction and fire swept through the dry grass of the nesting grounds. Pesticides did the rest.

By 1979, only six dusky seaside sparrows could be found along the river. Five of them were captured. None were females. The last female had been sighted in 1975.

The New York Times duly noted the problem in the August 31, 1983, edition under a headline that read: "Five Sparrows, All Male, Sing for a Female to Save Species." And just below the *Times* article, in one of those ethereal juxtapositions that sometimes occur in newspaper layouts, was an advertisement for a chichi clothing store called Breakaway. The copy above a photo of a smartly-turned-out woman went like this:

You strive for spontaneity
To take life as it comes
The perfect complement to your dynamic lifestyle
Our natural silver fox jacket

Now during our Labor Day celebration
Save $1000.00 off the original price
Originally $3990.00, now $2990.00

In the swamps of Florida, spontaneity was on hold. So were dynamic lifestyles. The five male duskies were brought to Disney World's Discovery Island, were pensioned off and made comfortable. Orange Band was about eight years old.

So it was, not far from the place where we launch for other worlds, that a different kind of countdown began. By 1985, there were three of the little males left. Then one died in September of that year. On March 31, 1986, a second one died. That left Orange Band, by himself.

Now and then, I would think of Orange Band alone in his cage. The last member of the rarest species known to us. He became blind in one eye, became old for a sparrow, and yet he persisted, as if he knew his sole task was to sustain the bloodline as long as possible. I wondered if he wondered, if he felt sorrow, or excruciating panic at the thought of his oneness. Surely he felt loneliness. Charles Cook, curator of the zoo, issued periodic bulletins: "As far as we can tell, for a little bird like that he seems to be doing fine."

Still it was inevitable. On June 18, 1987, a *Washington Post* headline said: "Goodbye, Dusky Seaside Sparrow." Orange Band, blind in one eye, old and alone, was gone. He died by himself on June 17th, with no one, either human or bird, around.

But the day Orange Band died there was a faint sound out there in the universe. Hardly noticeable unless you were expecting it and listening. It was a small cry, the last one, that arched upward from a cage in Florida, ricocheted along galactic highways and skimmed past the scorched parts of an old moon rocket still in orbit. If you were listening closely, though, you could hear it . . . "I am zero."

Extinct. The sound of the word is like the single blow of a hammer on cold steel. And each day the hammer falls again as another species becomes extinct due to human activity. This is about 400 times the rate of natural extinction. Norman Meyers has projected that, by the end of this century, species will be vanishing at the rate of 100 per day.

In open defiance of the International Whaling Commission, Japan and Iceland continue to slaughter whales under the guise of "research." The real reason, however, is to supply the inexhaustible Japanese appetite for whale flesh. The great California condors are all in cages now.* Less than twenty of the black-footed ferrets remain. The number of mountain gorillas has declined to under 450. The black duck is in serious trouble; nobody knows just how much trouble for sure. Over six million dolphins have been killed accidentally by the Pacific tuna fleet the last thirty years. And have you noticed the decline of songbirds in Iowa?

The count rises, year after year. Roughly eleven hundred plants and animals are identified specifically on the endangered and threatened species list at the present time, but nobody really knows for sure how long the list

*Several have been released back into the wild, as of 1993.

should be. The reason is that science has not yet determined exactly how many species exist, and the job of identification is a long way from completion. With the clear-cutting of the tropical rain forests throughout the world, the numbers could be astronomical. For example, the current rate of forest loss is two hundred thousand square kilometers per year, and some estimates of species yet unknown in the tropical forests range as high as one million.

But we press on. With highways and toxic waste and all-terrain vehicles and acid rain and pesticides and the straightening of pretty creeks to gain an extra acre or two on which to grow surplus crops. In the name of progress and something called "development," we press on, though we seem reluctant to define exactly what it is we seek. That definition, you see, likely is too frightening to contemplate, for the answer along our present course might be nothing other than "more."

More of what? Nothing in particular. Just more. We must have more, always more, for if we stopped, we would have less of that nothing in particular.

So the citizens buzz over blood and money around the boxing rings of Atlantic City and worry, ludicrously, about holding wineglasses properly and titter in a breathless way over Cher's ruthlessly salacious gown at the Academy Award ceremonies. And each day the hammer falls again. And each day another small cry arches upward; slowly and forever it arches upward. And sometimes I sit with my back against a granite ledge, near a river in a distant twilight colored blue, and say, "I am Orange Band," and the words come back alone through the trees and along the grass.

116

Drinking Wine
the New York Way

Just when I was settling comfortably into my middle years, confident that I possessed a certain stock of savoir faire acquired from decades of living and travel, comes now Diane Roupe to remind me of how far I have yet to go. In one of those punchy and informative articles common to newspaper society pages, *The Des Moines Register* published a piece on June 29, 1988, that contained directions for holding a wineglass properly.

Originally published in *The Des Moines Register*, July 8, 1988.

117

It seems that Ms. Roupe, formerly of Des Moines and lately of New York, has returned to her home, awaiting what the article labeled "career developments." While awaiting, she became aware that Iowans might not be handling their wineglasses properly and decided to set us straight.

And, I must tell you, it was a shock. There I was, drinking coffee at 6 A.M., awaiting developments in my career, and mulling over the choice between wearing my dirty blue canvas shirt or my "How 'bout Them Hogeyes" T-shirt, when I chanced upon the interview with Ms. Roupe. Stunned at the apparent deficiencies in my repertoire of deportment when amidst polite company, I read the article with near reverence. Nay, more than that, I was riveted by her words.

Then I immediately checked with Stanley Walk at the Sportsman's Lounge in St. Ansgar to see if he had read and understood the instructions. He was smashing a hole through the wall of the establishment he and Allen Kruger operate and had difficulty hearing me over the phone. It turns out, though, he had missed the article and implored me to repeat the core ideas for the benefit of his customers. That, and my unceasing interest in improving the lot of all Iowans, compels me to provide here the essence of Ms. Roupe's wisdom. Now pay attention, this gets complicated.

DO NOT: Do not place two fingers and the thumb at the bottom of a wineglass bowl, with the last two fingers holding the stem. That used to be just dandy, but not anymore. This is known as the Marlene Dietrich Caress, and IT IS DEFINITELY OUT.

DO: Do place four fingers on one side of the stem and your thumb on the other side (never allow your thumb to stop touching the stem for more than five seconds). Such a grip prevents a premature warming of the wine due to your hand and also enables you to grasp the glass securely, according to Ms. Roupe. This is the Distinguished New York Authorities Clamp, and IT IS IN.

I know, I know, change is difficult. I whined at first, too. After all, old habits are notoriously hard to break. I learned my drinking skills from emulating guys such as Red and Corny and Zip and Lefty in my Iowa youth. All of them dictated, by example, the standards of proper etiquette to be followed while sipping from assorted containers in the bowling alleys and taverns of Rockford. Sometimes they were kind enough to offer exhibitions right on the street, usually late of a Saturday evening. And with only minimal persuasion, Lefty and the others would gladly move into more advanced techniques, such as the proper handling of quart bottles and gallon jugs.

Yet, Diane Roupe assures us that such a revision in our drinking manners is critical. She even manages to tie the new, and admittedly difficult, glass grasp into economic development. The syllogism runs as follows: Industry wants to locate in sophisticated surroundings;

Iowans will be seen as sophisticated if we hold our wine-glasses correctly; therefore, etc., etc. In other words, just wait and see if those silly old companies will move here unless we clean up our social act.

That piece of logic alone settles the issue and ensures rapid adoption of the new grip by all right-thinking Iowans. Remember Groucho Marx's duck that used to come down from the ceiling when people said the magic word on "You Bet Your Life"? That entitled the players to a bonus. Say "economic development" in Iowa, and the duck descends like the value of farmland after a speculative binge. The universities picked up on that right away.

But wait! There's more. Beer and highballs are out, and ordering either of those in a fine restaurant, according to Ms. Roupe, will definitely identify you as not being a New Yorker. I'm having trouble with this part. If a Brooklyn cabdriver goes to the Café Carlyle to hear Bobby Short and orders a Pabst, does that mean he's not from New York?

There are other things that will identify you as not being a New Yorker also, though Ms. Roupe did not point them out. Since she believes that people from Iowa will want to emulate the good manners of New Yorkers, I will provide several more guides for behavior when you visit the ol' Apple. For example, if you know the names and locations of all the states and have a fair idea of what transpires in each of them, you'll immediately be identified as not being a sophisticated New Yorker. This is particularly true if you know that Idaho grows potatoes. So, be careful.

Here's another example. You will not pass for a New Yorker if you dislike pieces of styrofoam pasted on yellow cardboard displayed in art galleries and selling for $27,542. Likewise, be careful of criticizing kitsch photography done in sort of an art deco style, featuring boring pictures of bored surburban couples sitting by bored backyard swimming pools. Be sure you like these photographs or you will be OUT.

Obviously, I'm joshing a little bit. We all agree that Iowans are not as well turned out socially as they might be, and there are serious questions that were not covered in the article. Here is a partial list of dilemmas that I hope will be answered in future interviews with Ms. Roupe:

Is balancing a wineglass on your nose or head okay? Or is that permissible only at the end of world wars?

Why are there sometimes two wine lists—one bound in leather and the other in plastic?

If you like to hold your glass down along your pant leg, what is the correct grip?

What is the proper grasp if you prefer your wine at body temperature?

New York waiters yank my wineglass from the table and pay more attention to other patrons right after I say, "Gimme a Bud." Why?

121

Iowans chill their wine to just above freezing. Does this have any effect on the right way to hold a glass?

How about those plastic champagne glasses where the stem detaches from the bowl? What is to be done here?

Why do busboys often err and put a fork at the top of my plate, perpendicular to the other flatware? Should I refuse to tip the waiter when this occurs or should I just cackle and point?

Why doesn't my van get better gas mileage?

Well, it's apparent that a whole new vista is opening for the *Register*. To paraphrase photographer Galen Rowell, many Iowans come, looking, looking. And we need directions while we're looking, looking, so that we will never be mistaken for Iowans while mingling with the tonier elements of New York society. God forbid such confusion and its impact on economic development. Thus, we will continue to seek guidance from our newspaper wherein our arbiters of taste will instruct us in model behavior. The next article in the series will deal with how to keep score in tennis.

Oh yes, in line with this new thrust toward Iowa chic, Messieurs Walk and Kruger will begin offering wineglass-holding classes on August 1 at the Sportsman's Lounge (students must bring their own glasses, preferably clean). I advise other such establishments to consider similar instruction if you want to be part of a future Iowa. The duck is falling.

I think I'll stop. Writing nasty things about such nonsense is on the same order of difficulty as nailing guppies to plywood and hitting them with roofing hammers. I'm sorry to be quite so blunt, Ms. Roupe, but I have other work. You see, children are dying in the Sudan from disease and hunger. Then there's acid rain, water pollution, soil erosion, the mistreatment of animals, child abuse, drug addiction, race relations, toxic waste disposal, the clear-cutting of the Amazon basin, students to be taught, and so forth. Besides, once the Arabs get their act together, New York will cease to exist.

But I am troubled by a single thought. I try to reject it, yet I cannot. In a world that pays so little attention to the things that ought to matter and focuses instead on the trivial fringes of what it means to be civilized, truly civilized, I must admit to the following: Diane Roupe is probably right. And God help us all.

In Cedar Key,
Harriet Smith Loves Birds
and Hates Plastic

When Harriet Smith told her boss she was quitting her job and moving to Florida to write a novel, he offered her three months' paid leave and psychiatric help. By contemporary standards, his reaction was understandable. Harriet was selling $5 million worth of computers each year to high-level corporate executives. She was the personification of what is supposed to be the modern woman's dream, slugging it out and moving up fast in a glamour industry.

Originally published in *The Des Moines Register*, March 3, 1989.

That was six years ago. And Harriet wanted neither a paid leave nor psychiatric help. She wanted to be free. So she chucked it all, sold just about everything she owned, loaded her ten-year-old son in a camper, and headed south from New Hampshire. She was running hard, escaping from a world where time is measured in nanoseconds, where worth is judged by the crackle of the bank check and the close of the sale. She never looked back.

Now it's late afternoon on the Florida gulf coast, and the long swamp grass behind her house turns a soft yellow-green in the fading light. Twenty feet away at her Cedar Key Seabird Rescue, brown pelicans recuperating from various injuries flap around in a large confinement. Harriet Smith leans forward, rests her chin on her hands, and says, "I want to open up people's heads and pour some things in there."

It took her a while to find herself and this half-acre in the Florida scrub country. She wandered around Florida for three years, south to the Keys and then north once more. By 1983, Harriet was living in Tallahassee, picking oranges and painting houses, doing some writing on the side. But the novel went poorly, so she tried plays and short stories, then articles. None of it caught on.

She drifted down to Cedar Key where the wild beauty of Levy County took hold of her. And, sitting on a bench along Second Street, she decided this was her place. While launching her painting business in a new market, she worked as a waitress at the Island Hotel, a place of quiet fame among those who seek gourmet food and similar comforts.

Harriet's Cedar Key Seabird Rescue started with an injured brown pelican on the beach. The story is a common one along the coast—five fishhooks embedded in various parts of the bird's body and monofilament line wrapped so tightly around a grotesquely swollen leg that the line itself disappeared within the swelling.

She waited four hours for a busy wildlife officer to respond to her call. And Harriet Smith, waitress and house painter, spent that time watching over the pelican and raging within herself at her own ignorance about what might be done to help. She remembers making herself a promise: "Never again, never, am I going to have this helpless feeling."

An internship at the Suncoast Seabird Center south of Clearwater gave her some basic knowledge. A correspondence course in bird biology from Cornell University added to it. But most of what Harriet knows about birds has come from the day-to-day caring for them. She disdains the more clinical, drug-oriented approach of many bird veterinarians and labels her approach to bird medicine as "holistic."

Harriet's landlord in Cedar Key initially was tolerant. But the birds and cages and dead fish and droppings in his backyard finally wore him down. So, now what?

The situation presented her with a moral dilemma. You see, when Harriet Smith left the computer business, she had made up her mind to be poor. "I decided that I always was going to be poor, that I was never going to own property, that I was never going to own a new car again, never get a bank loan, and never have a checking account." When she talks like that, you can feel the foun-

127

dations quake just a little, and folks in the chrome and glass houses along the southern beaches probably sense a sudden chill in the wind and wonder about its origin.

Yet there had to be a place for the birds. So she compromised a little with the system and scraped together $400 for a down payment on a small piece of land near Cedar Key. She makes her monthly payments of $83.68 directly to the previous owner. The tallyman again, but no banks at least.

Connie Nelson, friend and local artist, ramrodded a modest fund-raising push on Harriet's behalf. "Okay everybody, $5 each for Harriet's Seabird Rescue Center." Harriet was under way.

She built her own house, a small L-shaped affair, mostly out of donated materials. Well, "built" is a little too strong, too finished. The house is sort of emerging here and there as funds permit. The posts supporting the structure are not on the square, but that bothers her little. "My great-grandfather lived in a house like this; it wasn't square, it didn't fall down, and he was very happy. You have to get away from the kind of mind-set that worries about those things." Well said and noted.

"Everything for the house seems to come in $300 chunks," she moans. "Everything costs that much, for some reason." The next $300, whenever she accumulates it, will go for a well. For now, she hauls water in buckets from Cedar Key.

After that, maybe a better electricity setup. Her only supply of electrical power is carried by two extension cords running from a temporary construction electric pole. One cord goes to the house, the other to a freezer containing food for the birds.

But her private war against suffering is what really matters. She finances that and her own expenses by working part-time as a desk clerk in a local motel, by writing an environmental column for the *Cedar Key Beacon*, and by selling copies of her book, *A Naturalist's Guide to Cedar Key, Florida*.

As people learn of her work, donations trickle in. Some of the money comes from local folks, some from people in Pocatello and Minneapolis who own property in Cedar Key, subscribe to the *Beacon*, and read her column.

She spent $1,250 on her birds last year. She figures $3,000 a year would permit a first-class operation by enabling her to build better confinements, purchase higher-quality food for the birds, and acquire additional training for herself. Her monetary needs seem shriveled in comparison with the large government grants regularly handed out to academic researchers. Without degrees and credentials, though, she feels that kind of money is beyond her reach. "*Crud*entials," she sighs.

No matter. Harriet Smith is an expert at making do. Conventional thinking has it that high levels of purchasing by some swirling mass of procuring organisms called "consumers" are necessary to the well-being of the U.S. economic system. If you believe that, then you probably will find Harriet a little dangerous. By example, she is subversive in a gentle fashion.

Harriet watches the rise and fall of life in the marsh to the east through windows that were given to her. In fact, most of the house is constructed of scraps and discards. Sometimes she'll return home and find a used door propped on the stoop. Or the phone rings and someone asks, "I have an old water heater. Do you have any use for it?" "Sure, bring it out; I'll convert it to a solar water heater."

So what's the point of it all? What's it mean in the long run? Harriet is quick to respond to such patently stupid questions. "Most of the animals are injured by some human activity," she observes. "In some tiny way, ever so slightly, I tip the scales the other way. I talk about birds anywhere, anytime. People become aware of the birds, know their names, and call me when they see injured birds. Once that starts happening, people become more aware of what they've got here in Levy County; they realize how special it is."

She sees Levy County as one of the last few wilderness areas in Florida. "It's eleven hundred square miles, and it's absolutely fabulous. Essentially every habitat in Florida is here. I sometimes think, 'Fence off Levy County.' "

As part of her bird lectures and columns, she actively promotes her own brand of hard-headed environmentalism. Plastic is one of her favorite targets—she absolutely loathes plastic. "It doesn't work to tell people they ought to recycle and not use so much plastic. You've got to show them how. 'Here,' I tell them, 'here are five ways to stop using so much plastic.' I go to the grocery store and say, 'Don't give me those damn plastic bags. What's the matter with you, Harry? Why do you have

130

those things?' " Fearing a full-blown lecture, Harry shakes his head and reaches for something else, anything.

It's early evening now, and the flashing cursors on all those computer terminals are far behind her. They blink somewhere in another time. Harriet feeds a small eastern screech owl recovering from a broken leg and an eye injury. The little guy's beak clicks rapidly in anticipation as he waits for her to prepare his ration of stew meat marinated in a vitamin solution.

While she feeds him, Harriet looks out across the scrub tree horizon. Out there, she knows, the white ibises, the yellow-billed cuckoos, the ducks and owls and eagles and ospreys and the rest are up against the power of a technology-choked civilization, and they are losing.

She knows that out there the birds are flying into utility wires, eating mercury-laden fish, and slamming into automobiles. And out there in the island rookeries and along the beaches, the wry and earnest pelicans are tangled in the trees and hobbling along the sand, fighting the fish hooks and monofilament line.

So Harriet Smith works through the Florida days alone. She's trying to get $300 together for a well. Trying to buy better-quality food for her birds and to find a home for a brown pelican with only one wing. Trying to open up our heads and pour some sensibility in there. She's trying to tip the scales ever so slightly. Not much, just a little bit.

POSTSCRIPT

Harriet operated her seabird rescue center from 1987 to 1991. Eventually, she just plain wore out, trying to earn a living as a house painter while caring for and supporting the birds at the same time. The range of species at her center had expanded, and she was spending $25 a week on meat for her birds and animals. There came a moment when she stood looking at a red fox, a barred owl, and a Cooper's hawk. All of them were meat eaters. The choice had come to this: feed them or feed herself. She closed the rescue center.

I saw Harriet recently. She looks better, not so tired. She's running the Cedar Key Book Store on C Street and conducting two-hour boat trips as a naturalist. On Friday mornings she gives talks on the natural aspects of Cedar Key. What about the birds, the animals? Several people in town have permits to transport injured creatures to other places where they can be cared for.

Harriet figures it would have taken $10,000 a year to keep the rescue center open. That would have allowed her to buy the proper equipment she needed, hire an assistant, and provide food for the birds and animals. But the money wasn't there. It's never there for the important things. I thought about that as I walked along the streets of Cedar Key on a quiet morning in February of 1993. I thought about it while I watched pelicans coming in from the islands and saw new condos going up along the shore.

Brokerage

Stanley Walk and Allen Kruger, proprietors of the Sportsman's Lounge and related enterprises in St. Ansgar, go unbounded. They subscribe not to limits and are unmoved by small-town demands for convention. Moreover, even in our darker times, they believe in Iowa and have little patience with those who feel otherwise. So, to them, it seemed perfectly natural to have an autograph party at the tavern to celebrate the publication of a new book dealing with Iowa.

Originally published in *One Good Road Is Enough*, 1990.

133

Now, those of delicate, patrician tastes might see contradictions, or at least curious impropriety, in this idea—books and taverns and all. Not Stanley Walk, not Allen Kruger. "Get the author to commit, and we'll handle the rest," they said to the Iowa State University Press. "All right, let's do it," the author replied. Up went the flyers in the grocery stores of Worth and Mitchell counties. Arrange a radio interview on one of the local stations with the author. Get announcements on television and in the papers. Post signs, talk about it, plan and promote.

The weather turned rough in early November. Snow squalls throughout the day of the signing. Cold, and windy, and wet. The boys playing cards at the big circular table in the back never did figure out what was going on. By ten in the morning, there were piles of new books in plastic shrink-wrap stacked on a table. Some guy with long, gray hair—probably a liberal, the card players guessed—showed up with a pen and started signing copies of the book for people from such alien civilizations as Osage, Mason City, Fort Dodge, smaller Iowa towns, and southern Minnesota.

At lunch, a choice of beef or chicken, the author read an essay from the book to forty people who had paid $7.50 to eat and listen. One of them, a veterinarian, said, "It was a religious experience." The author's mother sat at the head table and recognized all the people in the story, herself included.

By afternoon, on a Saturday in early winter, it was a tableau straight out of everybody's vision of how America ought to be. Part Norman Rockwell, part Thomas Jefferson. In booths along the wall and tables down the middle, people were sitting quietly, drinking coffee or sipping a beer, reading the book.

For some reason, a number of political figures, elected and otherwise, had shown up. Their presence resulted in a kinetic discussion of what those folks like to call "issues," along with an impromptu strategy session for last-minute campaigning. Proponents of keeping Brushy Creek just the way it is, in the face of threats to build a dam in the wilderness area, arrived, commandeered a booth, and argued their cause to all who would listen. Next to them, other folks were planning a conference on rivers. The author signed more books, and the boys playing cards at the big circular table in the back were getting even more confused, swiveling around between hands just to keep track of things.

Among the guests was the author's high school typing teacher. While signing her book, he reflected that she probably had as much to do with getting the book finished as anyone else. An Osage man claimed that he and several other hunters had sworn off goose hunting after reading one of the author's polemics on the subject. Upon hearing that, the author offered to print "Civilized Adult" across the man's forehead, but that was judged to be unwise, somewhat overdone.

KGLO television, from Mason City, clanked in with cameras and cords, requesting an interview with the author. The man with the questions wanted to talk about economic development and computers; the author wanted to talk about shooting pool and rivers.

Snow blew down the main street of St. Ansgar as a fortyish woman with silver hair and a nice smile pur-chased a book and covertly inquired, "How can I get you to read the rest of the book to me?" The author replied, "Just ask, I'm easy." Mike, whose last name disappeared along with a scrap of paper, wants to show the author secret places along the Cedar River. Great. Spring will be perfect for that.

Stanley Walk beamed, served the customers, and carried more books from his office to the signing table. Allen Kruger argued politics. Stanley and the author talked about a poetry reading at the tavern, with maybe some music to go along with it. Sounds good. It'll get done sometime. By 3:30, the demand for literary sustenance was tapering off. The author packed up his pen, and his mother, and drove south along blacktop roads, while the politicos stayed behind to discuss issues and, in Shakespeare's words, figure out how to "circumvent God."

Stanley calls with the tally. Ninety-six books were sold that day. That's nice, but slightly irrelevant, not what's important here. The point is there are people out there who write or play music or do theater or create visual beauty or have problems to discuss. And there are people out there who want to read the words or listen to the music or see things of beauty or participate in the solving of nasty dilemmas. The predicament is one of brokerage, of getting all those folks together.

It can be done. Stanley Walk and Allen Kruger did it, and life became a little richer for everyone concerned because of it. The ideal of a literate, caring, sensitive, and participative society is attainable, at least in Iowa. All that's required is a little brokerage. We proved that on a snowy November day in St. Ansgar.

136

Running into Perry

Do you remember Perry
Burgess? I'm his brother." I had just autographed a book
for a man in a Marshalltown, Iowa, store and looked up.

Of course I remembered Perry. Instantly I could
see him, forty years back along the cambers of my recollections. Dusty flatlands afternoon, high summer, Rockford, Iowa. Perry in work boots and cutoff jeans, shirtless,
red bandanna tied around his head, good muscles. Slightly

Originally published in *One Good Road Is Enough*, 1990.

untamed and pretty close to what the counterculture folks looked like two decades later.

Perry, though, was permitted his quirks. Even in the hairy-chested culture of rural Iowa, where short pants on men were considered a telltale sign of unsteady masculinity. He was special, you see. He could handle the pounding heat of the kilns at the brick-and-tile plant in summer. As I recall, not many could. Maybe just him. He monopolized stamina. And that counted for something. Allowances could be made for Perry.

He carried his head at a slight angle; a bad eye might have caused that. Perry grinned a lot in those days, grinned at kids like me on the street in my old sneakers and jeans. I grinned back. I liked Perry. I liked his toughness and his style. I liked his good humor in the face of the brutal days he spent in the kilns. My mother has always remarked that my heroes were, well, a little different from those of other boys. I liked Kenny Govro, cat fisherman; Sammy Patterson, billiards player; and I liked Perry Burgess, kiln stacker.

When the annual softball game between the local merchants and the plant workers came around, it was understood Perry would be on the mound. "Perry 'The Dipsy-Doodler' Burgess." That's what he liked to be called in the weeks preceding the game. That's how the cardboard signs advertising the game listed him. That's what the local newspaper called him in announcements.

"Satch." He also liked to be called "Satch." I think that flowed from his respect for Satchel Paige, the great baseball pitcher. "Hey, Satch!" we'd yell at Perry Burgess. "Ready for the game?" He'd cock his head and grin.

138

Actually, he wasn't much of a pitcher. Given Perry's style, that was not the point. Under the lights of a country ball diamond, he pitched wildly, wheeled and dealt with seventeen different motions. Threw the ball behind his back, between his legs, the crowd roaring in approval. Old men in the stands whacked each other on the back and croaked, "That Perry Burgess, he sure is somethin' isn' he?"

On the mound, way out there in the dust with Satchel Paige riding his shoulder, Perry cocked his head and grinned at the applause, careened into his windup, and delivered another dipsy-doodler in the general direction of home plate. From kiln stacker to softball jester in three hours. Perry had range, that much was certain.

"Sure I remember Perry," I said out loud to his brother, Albert Burgess. "I'd love to see him again." "Well, he's right over there, sitting on a bench." Albert motioned, and across the floor of an Iowa shopping mall came Perry Burgess. Small, old, head cocked, grinning. I loomed over him, tall, taller than he'd ever been back there in the dusty days.

We shook hands. I grinned and told him about my feelings: "You were one of my heroes." Grabbing the book I had already signed, I wrote Perry's name in it, along with something about the esteem I held for him back down the years. I wanted to talk more, but there were books to be autographed, a stack of them. The holiday traffic was heavy. Christmas music over the sound system. Perry and his brother drifted off, politely.

But I was warmed by seeing Perry again. Old feelings, good feelings. In my boyhood, Perry Burgess was one of the eagles and made those days better in ways still undefinable. Maybe it had to do with style, with flaunting convention and getting away with it. I don't know; it doesn't matter. The years run, but some of the old heroes are still out there, and I am comforted by that.

A few months later, in the summer, I wandered through the ruins of the tile plant. Weeds and trees have taken back the spaces where hard men worked the clay. There are spirits in that place. You'd have to be less than a quarter sentient not to feel them, to hear the shouts and footsteps, hear the freight cars rolling down the spur.

I came to the kilns. Three of them, with doors open, round and domed and thirty feet in diameter. Hornet nests in the cracks, dust blowing across the floors.

Sweating, August hot, I stood in one of the kilns for a moment, thinking of Perry. The image of an old man in a Marshalltown shopping mall was gone. That's not the way I see him. Nope. Not at all. This way: boots, cutoff jeans, no shirt, red bandanna around his head, good muscles. "Hey, Satch! Ready for the game?" Head slightly cocked, grinning, on the street outside of the beer joints, on the mound. That's how I remember Perry.

The ol' Dipsy-Doodler, out there under the lights, sliding into his windup, delivering. Darn right I remember him. He was important to me. Still is. It was good running into Perry.

The Lion of Winter

*F*elis concolor, middle-brown in the thin light of a winter afternoon, comes out of the scrub thirty feet ahead of me, three hundred yards from the Pacific. She crosses the old Park Service road in easy strides and, without hesitating, takes her one hundred pounds into a soft curving leap over a patch of low brush on the other side, like a house cat arching into a cardboard box.

Instinctively then, I am into a crouch and turning

Originally published in *One Good Road Is Enough*, 1990.

to the woman behind me. "Did you see the lion?" I say quietly. "What?" she answers, confused. "The mountain lion, the cougar, did you see it?"

For a moment she doesn't believe me. I can tell. Another of my little stories, she thinks; the outdoor man teasing the indoor woman again. From my shoulder comes the knapsack, and I dig frantically within it for a camera. "A what? Where?" the woman asks again, earnestly. I tell her and begin to move slowly up the narrow and abandoned road, toward the place where the cat has gone into the brush.

Only two miles behind, the van rests on a highway's edge. Back there is air-conditioning and speed, concrete and the road to cities. Here, the technological ground is different, tilted a bit in favor of the lion. And, in some curious way, I relish that. She is at home, and I am the stranger. A kind of interspecies democracy has taken hold, and my place in the food chain seems less secure than it did a few minutes ago.

Staring hard, my eyes watering from the energy of focus, I reach the brush and look into it. Nothing. Farther up the road in quiet steps, I stop and look long into the grass and brambles. Nothing.

Disappointed and turning toward the woman, I catch the breath of her whisper on the wind of late afternoon: "It's here. It's right here." She looks back into the tangle, then at me, partly confused, partly afraid.

Carefully, I go back along the road, my boots silent on old dirt, until I stand beside the woman and look where she is looking. And there is the face, a young one but old enough to be on her own, looking back at me from ten feet away—the eyes yellow-green, white fur around the mouth and chin, whiskers silver-gray in the mottled light, ears pointing up.

For a moment, just a moment, the eyes of order Carnivora and order Primates come together. I look at her. She stares back, unblinking. Then, perhaps catching a faint and lingering smell of the spear, she is gone, not even as a shadow, but rather like the dream of one. No branch flickering, no crackling of brush, no sound at all.

In the ways only cats are given, she just swings her head, moves off, and leaves us standing there along a road, by a river, near the sea. The one frame of film I remember to shoot as she goes eventually develops into a brown, out-of-focus blur. I will throw it in the discard box. The memory of such things is always better than a photograph, anyhow.

The woman and I move on toward the sea, talking of lions and yellow-green eyes and the wondrous good fortune of seeing the cat. Just the night before we had been driving along a mountain road, headlights sweeping thick forest on the curves, and I had said, "There are only a few things I need to do yet in my life; one of them is to see a mountain lion in the wild." So we talk about that and other matters of chance.

As we walk toward the beach, I am silent about the fact that big cats have been known to follow humans, if only out of some passing curiosity. Now and then, however, I glance backward along the path and into the trees. Truly, though, we have little to fear. The number of attacks on humans by mountain lions statistically is low. But, as one biologist has pointed out, mountain lions can't count. Later, I tell an official from the Mountain Lion Coalition about our meeting with the cat, and she says, "Do you realize how special that is?" I do. The probability of such an encounter is incredibly small. The big cats, nocturnal and secretive, are twilight figures even to those who seek to study them.

Except for thirty or so Florida panthers, and their survival is tenuous, the eastern lands are pretty much empty of lions. Killed as vermin or game or their habitat destroyed, they have gone. Though some believe that the cougars or pumas or mountain lions or catamounts, all of them the same animal, are moving back into remote areas of New England, northern Minnesota, and Michigan as forests regenerate and the deer population increases.

Aside from the perverse human tendency to destroy anything that offers the least bit of threat, the loss of range is the true vandal of the cougar's world. They are the ultimate individualists, loners except at mating time, and the consummate travelers, requiring a space of forty to two hundred square miles for their hunting.

Their range, particularly in the Far West, unceasingly falls to the saw and the highway and the condominium. California alone has lost 7.7 million acres of lion habitat since the 1800s, 4.5 million of those acres since 1945.

Moreover, as with all cats, the lions are uncooperative, even when humans are trying to help them. Estimates of the lion population are disputed vigorously among various groups interested in the cougar's preservation. The truth is that nobody knows for sure how well or poorly the lions are faring, and the big cats aren't talking.

Still, I had that moment. And I claim as much for it as any of the things I have seen. I have looked into the eyes of a starlight traveler whose lands recede steadily now. So, like the wild spaces themselves, I also grow less in contemplating a world too small and too selfish and too beset upon the trivial and transitory for the allowance of freedom, freedom that is colored middle-brown in the light of a winter day and carefully must keep to ever-diminishing cover.

I sigh within myself at the losses we sustain, the cat and I, for each of us understands in our own fashion that range, free range, is the way to the center of things. To take that from a traveler is to take all—from the traveler, from ourselves. And freedom thus becomes not even like a shadow, but rather like the dream of one. Like a dream I once had out along the edge of the great ice, a long time ago, before wisdom came and, along with other childish things, I put the spear aside.

One Good Road
Is Enough

Autumn in 1949, night, and the geese are moving south. I hear them talking, toss the covers aside, and scramble to the foot of my bed, looking out the window. Low they are, coming down the river valley and passing over town. On unsleeping wings they ride, long necks extended, with sober eyes that see only time and far things and space . . . and me, I think.

They know I'm here, I'm sure of that. Ten-year-old boys have not yet succumbed to a world counseling

Originally published in *One Good Road Is Enough*, 1990.

consumption in place of laughter and duty in place of wings. The geese understand. I clutch the bed covers to my face, responding to some curious mixture of delight in their coming and sorrow at watching them pass.

Celestial reckoning. That's how they go ... by the stars. That's how they find the ponds of Texas. Scientists study their ways, dissecting and inducing. The answers will elude them. It's magic, and no one can argue me otherwise, at age ten or four decades later. Logic and data have their place, but not in the night, not out along the roads of wonder, where the music rises and the Canadas fly and a wizard waves them onward with long sweeps of his arm from tall grass in the river meadows.

I lie back on my pillow. My parents are asleep, but the little brown radio beside my bed, the one with only two dials and tan cloth covering over the speaker, glows in the darkness. "Welcome to 'Your Saturday Night Dance Party,'" the smooth baritone from New Orleans says. The music is live, and I know, absolutely, there are handsome men and beautiful women. They are eating and drinking, and dancing on a southern rooftop, a big hotel, their hair only slightly ruffled by a soft wind from the gulf.

Over the music and following the geese I hear a Rock Island freight train. In the bottomlands south of me, the wizard is laughing and does a backward flip, unable to contain himself. The Road is busy tonight—music from New Orleans, geese across the moon, trains across the trestle. The wizard loves the Road and is teaching me to love it, as both an illusion and a reality.

I fade in and out of sleep, wandering along the

edge of things, open to the possibilities. The music changes and images come. People dressed in wind-whipped black, carrying daggers with carved handles and drinking tea in front of flapping tents, waiting for the call to prayer. Camels moving silk and frankincense at a steady pace over blowing sand, pushing hard toward Medina. Near morning, my mother pulls the covers over me and turns off the little radio, while I travel, far from her.

There was only one good road leading out of Rockford, Iowa, back then. The rest were gravel, loose and dusty in the summer, treacherous in the winter. But one good road is enough. I knew that's all it took. I could travel east on it, go south on Highway 14, swing east again and catch one of the big highways leading down to New Orleans, or, for that matter, to Paris or Persia or twilight places in the Amazon Basin.

These were not fantasies without the possibility of fulfillment. I never believed that for a moment. They were plans, you see, plans that could be converted into small-town sidewalks that turned into streets that turned into highways and the highways into old steamers or airplanes or caravans headed toward market towns. The steady two-beat of a New Orleans drummer could become the complex syncopations of wrinkled hands on tightly stretched goatskin in high desert arroyos, and the Rock Island freight could some day be transformed into a long, chuffing train across Siberia. The images are the beginning; you must have the images first. Then comes the Road.

So I lean over a 4 A.M. hotel balcony in my forty-third year and watch Bombay work its way toward morning. Thirty-four hours in front of this, I had shut the front door of my house in Cedar Falls, slapped my vest pocket to make sure the tickets and passport were there, and picked up my suitcase. Car to the airport, commuter plane to Chicago, jet to New York, and there in the darkness was Air India 106, loading. Then London by daylight, and into the night again—Europe, Istanbul, Persia, the Gulf of Oman. India, unknown, and fearsome in that ignorance, out there somewhere.

On the balcony, I drink a Kingfisher beer as light approaches, watching Arab dhows run up their sails into the first wind of morning where the Portuguese once harbored, watching the street people cook their breakfast on charcoal burners, thinking of a little brown radio humming, geese flying, and a wizard promising me that my world would not always be so circumscribed as it was then.

I wander the streets of India. Touts offer sightseeing, drugs of any kind, and women, or young boys if a woman is not to my liking. I swim in a pool at dawn, listening to a flute somewhere, and fall in transient love with Indian women in green silk, gold upon their bodies. For seventeen nights I eat at a table next to that of Sir David Lean and his wife. He's here scouting locations for *A Passage to India*. We do not speak. My midwestern reticence and respect for privacy prevent me from asking about his dreams as a young boy. I know he thought of deserts and jungles and dark winds from Java, though.

And Arabia came along. On Themari Street in Riyadh, the old ways endure. There is gold, and women with covered faces and men with covered intentions.

There are calls to prayer and desert winds, and I wander through the markets at night looking for presents to take home. The bracelet will do, and the necklace. The scarf also. I flag down a taxi in the middle of a broad avenue. The driver is a Bedouin who remembers the sound of hooves and the taste of blowing sand. Far to the west, Canadas are beating their way south over the rooftops of northern Iowa.

Then Munich and Dubai and Hong Kong and Paris and on and on. I ride a coastal boat south of Puerto Vallarta to a fishing village. Staying there for a week without light or pure water, I listen to an African drummer tell me how the drums can talk, if you have the skill. I believe him and sit nearby while he plays to the darkness, on a hill 167 stone steps above the village. In the morning a man from San Francisco sings his night-dreams and invites others to do the same, while another man murmurs incantations to the beat of a smaller drum.

In the river towns of Belgium, winter lies hard and brittle upon me. Moving across the cold marble floors of a Flemish cathedral, I listen to the sound of my boot heels and wonder if the bishops in their crypts of stone are listening also. Was this the place? There's something here I can't touch, some ancient sense of having stood in these shadows before, and watched. Watched the lady in silver, small hurried steps as she came streaming down a secondary aisle past the confessionals and toward me. The image is there for a moment only. It wavers, dissolves, as early light comes through high and painted windows and colors orange a suffering Jesus, hanging, crucified.

151

St. Maarten is expensive, but the beaches are good. You can make up the cost at the casinos if you know blackjack and the cards are running your way. I am suspicious, though, about playing against the government. Governments think of gambling as taxes; they have unfavorable rules and close the casino while I'm in the middle of a streak. The hell with 'em. I put my winnings in a metal box at the hotel and catch the morning flight out of there. I'll try Macao next.

I ride long-tailed boats through the backwaters of Bangkok, hang off foggy cliffs in Acadia with my cameras, and follow snowy egrets through the swamps of south Georgia. In Big Sur, I read my poetry by firelight. There are professional poets with long hair in wide-brimmed hats, and pretty young women who love the idea of poets more than the words. The high plains drums are still there in New Mexico, if you listen, and old dogs lie in the streets of La Push, where violent January waves hammer the coast of northwestern Washington. A fusty woman, from Omaha twenty years back, combs the Oregon beaches and dreams of secret cargos only she will find. I spend an hour talking with her about that.

Now there is more than one good road out of Rockford, Iowa, though still only one to the east. The same one. I visit there and talk with my mother. She remembers the old brown radio, the one with two dials and a tan cloth covering over the little speaker. She remembers the late-night sound of geese overhead. But she never quite has understood the wizard or the Road or why the man she raised loves it so.

"India?" she says. "How many times will this

make?" "Three," I say. "There is more out there, and I'm fifty now. It's time for India again."

At some point, it gets down to "lasts." It's getting there now. I wear clothes for a long time. I wonder if my leather jacket, worn but tough, is the last one I'll buy. And my boots, good ones, Red Wings, are the same. The man at the shoe shop says they're going to outlive me. And my old hat? And the guitars? They'll go on forever. Maybe this is the last of the India voyages. Maybe.

I go down into the bottomlands to talk with the wizard of my summers. His ways are slanting ways, as mine have become and turn ever more so. He looks at the river purling by and listens to my questions. I ask again about the geese and the Road and the music, and what it all means. Where does it go from here? What about the "lasts"?

He is a fey companion, uneasy with too much directness, and begins to move away from me through meadow grass, chanting as he goes, his voice fading:

The High-Desert Master gave me a child
In return for some footprints
I found in the sand.
And I carried him here
Through fall and through winter
  Past old riders turning their ponies for summer,
  Past slavers who cried for their right to the boy,
  Past dancers who moved through the streets of Castile,
  Past arms reaching out from windows and doorways,
  Past women in black who were crying and offered
    Their only true daughters for a sigh and a drachma,

Past those who would counsel prudence and claimed
The dancers had gone and no more would follow,
Past old harbor seals who lay in the sunlight
And remembered the coming of Christ and before.
I carried him here to sweet meadows bending
And fought off the bandits who tried for his soul.
I gave him his love of sails leaving cover
And the sound of old flutes on the first wind of morning,
While I showed him the maps
Scribbled in chalk,
Washing away on the walls of September.
But women in green, with gold on their bodies,
Ah, they were the ones who took him away,
And gladly I gave him
Asking only one promise:

You must teach him to dance
In the twilight of Eden,
In the moments remaining,
Before it has gone.
For he is the last one
And

"Never again," cried the High-Desert Master.

"Never and never and never again."

Looking upward, he begins to sing, sweeping his
small arm in widening arcs. I follow the point of his
finger. Geese are moving south across a dagger-like slice
of moon, their ancient sextants working in sober eyes,

taking them along time and space, toward the ponds of Texas.

I drive my truck out of Rockford, down the one good road to the east. On the tape deck, Kitaro plays of blowing sand and loaded camels pushing hard toward red-walled cities in the deserts of Rajasthan. Goatskin drums underneath the melody. Switching over to celestial reckoning, I jam my boot harder on the accelerator, drifting somewhere between illusion and reality, refusing to succumb, thinking of magic . . . and believing in it.

Southern Flight

*Though boys throw stones at frogs in sport,
the frogs do not die in sport, but in earnest.*

— BION

I am twenty birds back on
the left side of the skein, looking over my shoulder at
Malachi. He has taken many pellets in his eastern wing
and cannot pull it high enough for a full stroke. My right
leg is dragging as we hammer our way south in the late
afternoon. Two pieces of shot are embedded there, and
they will cause me great difficulty when we land.

We stayed too long in the north. All of us knew
that. But the summer ran late and warm; we became fat,

Originally published in *The Des Moines Register*, October 23, 1988.

floated on amiable water, and delayed the leaving. Lobu had argued for days that it was time to go. But we whined or laughed at him and refused to rise when he urged us.

A cold night rain fell and turned to sleet by morning. We did not see four men take their places in long marsh grass when the sun was still far down the curve of Earth. At dawn, they began shooting while we were sleepy on the water.

Lobu sounded the lifting cry and was in the air at the first hint of camouflaged movement in the grass. I saw him begin to rise even before his warning slid across the pond. And I remember marveling at the great power of his young body, his wings taking him first along the water, then into a long curving roll as he fought for height and distance. I wondered if I had looked that splendid in my second year.

Others picked up the cry, and I knew this was more than Lobu's way of getting us moving. Amalo, one of the youngest geese, looked at me for a moment in panic and indecision. I signaled him instantly, reaffirming what he feared, and we began our takeoff, struggling desperately for speed, for another day, for another moment.

I called upon myself for the strength that once was there, I called upon myself for all that I had ever been. To my left, I could see a hunter swinging his dark barrel in a practiced even way, following the wife of Jonaku through early light.

Coming off the water she exploded in a cloud of blood and feathers as the full load hit her. Jonaku trembled when he went over her floating body only two feet below him. The hunters were firing shell after shell from pump guns, and I could see pellets digging into the water ahead of me.

East we all were moving, perpendicular to the guns, straight into a curious mixture of freezing rain and rising sun. Birds were tumbling downward, some giving cries, others falling only in silence. The guns kept firing as I reached climbing speed. Malachi had drawn almost even with me, coming up on my left as we passed directly in front of the muzzles.

Rolling upward to the right. Apricot flame. A surge of it. Buffeting cone of mountain thunder. At the same moment I felt the impact on my leg, Malachi shuddered and began to fall, but caught himself and stayed low behind a stand of tall grass where the guns could not find him.

Sixty yards out. Almost safe. Coming around to follow Lobu, I could see a cumbrous man sloshing through the water, a spaniel beside him. He was shouting a wild cry of exultation and waving his gun above his head; I did not understand his words.

Birds were struggling, others lay still. Sori paddled in small, tight circles, flopping randomly, a piece of shot in her brain, while the dog swam toward her. Zachary, the old one, was injured, but tried one more time to follow us. As he flailed wildly near the edge of the pond, a man in camouflage shot him again, and he died there on northern water.

I banked into a strong wind from the western lands and fell into place. Other birds were doing the same. Water streamed from our feathers and flashed in the light of Mother sun, while Lobu took us southward.

159

There are two great rivers in the middle of this land. We are flying sixty miles east of the one that flows from the Montana highlands, three hundred miles north of the Missouri lakes. Ahead on the point, Lobu is pushing us hard. He is angry with us for lingering so long at the pond of morning, and we know he is right to be angry. Seven birds were killed by the hunters.

Light snow is falling. The color of the sky matches Lobu's mood. Our cadence has been steady for the last seven hours, and we listen to the Words. Heard they are, but not spoken. The sound unfolds from the meter of our wings. There is a slight unevenness in our stroking, and it is from this that the Words arise.

Like a great pulsing sigh they come, sweeping back along the lines in which we fly. "Alooooom" is the sound. "Alooooom—We are One." It is our creed and our comfort.

The Words wash over me, and wondering about Malachi, I turn once more to look at him. I am startled to see blood coming from his left eye. I had not noticed the blood before, and I remember again that only his body saved me from the full load of shot. His good eye glitters with pain and desperation as he stares straight ahead, giving full energy to his flight.

Lobu is curving us around a tall structure with a round, dish-shaped plate at the top and over wires connected to it. We do not know the name of this thing, though we have seen many of them before.

Below, thin sheets of ice begin to form on shallow patches of water. The snow is falling with more intensity now, and each of us knows that we must keep moving. A blizzard would take many of us.

Ten yards across from me, in the western line, Shanta is also watching Malachi. They are old lovers. She feels an enduring warmth for him and tries to send some of her strength over the empty sky between them.

When I had younger wings, the long southern flight was exhilarating. There were many places to come down and rest at evening. Now the water has disappeared. From this height, we can see traces of primitive contours where once the marshes could be found.

They are gone now. To other things they are gone. To houses and planted fields and roads. And there is little left for us.

Much of the remaining water is surrounded by guns, preserved only for the killing, not for the good. It is said the hunters fight with their money and their time to save the marshlands, and, though we try, we find it difficult to be grateful. We do not understand the killing; we can only fly before it.

The young ones ask about the killing. "Why?" they ask. We have no answers, for there seem to be none. Once there were reasons, the very old ones say, but those reasons disappeared long before the marshes died.

"But," the young ones press us, "if not for the meat, then why? And why have they taken the marshes if they want our flesh? It makes no sense!"

In those moments, we would turn to Zachary. He had lifted in terror from many ponds, had fought for the safety of altitude through a thousand magenta dawns with buckshot lacing the red face of Mother sun, had seen the waters smeared with blood and lifeless birds floating on silent mornings, had counted in his years the disappearance of the places for living. Finally he would speak, but only after the young ones could not be quieted with generalities and platitudes.

"I have no way of understanding the thoughts of humans. I can only repeat what has come down to me through the elders. The origins of what I will tell you are shrouded by the failure of memories and the embellishment of time. I know only that the words were given by one of many forms who rested on a long sandbar in summer firelight and spoke in a tongue that knew no boundaries. When the elders asked the same questions that you now ask about the ways of humans, they were cautioned to listen, to remember. And the traveler spoke thusly":

> Ancient dreams, there are,
> Unresolved.
> And lingering impulses
> From the days of rocks and fire,
> Just after the great ice had gone.
> A reluctance to come before
> Themselves and ask,
> "Who are we, and what is our place
> Among all things?"
>
> An avoidance, there is,
> Of eternal questions,
> Difficult and submerged.

Questions yielding not to
Force but only to
Subtle strands of
Intelligence and feelings
Woven full and pure
Into a cloth that
Catches the soft wind
Of enlightenment
Like a billowing,
Saffron-colored sail
Upon an endless river.

The answers are feared
So the questions are scuttled.
For the answers,
If they are firm
And truly given,
Would require change.
Those who profit now
Would profit less.

Enlightenment
Gives rise to
Kindness
And
Simplicity
And
Quietude.
Little profit
Can be found
In any of those.

And, like yourselves on a
Warm autumn day,
When it seems the
Croupier can be denied
Forever,
They are reluctant
To rise.

With that, he would swim away and pretend to
busy himself at feeding along a shore where the wild rice
yet grew. We will miss Zachary.

Word has traveled far, and we have heard about
the condor and the falcon. And the little sparrows of the
Florida swamps. We have seen the canvasbacks lan-
guishing and the streams turning dark with soil from the
fields. The places for living are being taken or sullied
with poison.

Behind me, I hear a small sound. I turn to look at
Malachi and see his damaged wing flapping out of har-
mony with the good one. There is more blood coming
from his injured eye. Fear screams from the other. He
begins to fall away.

I start to follow him, but clearly he is gone. His
bad wing no longer is stroking, and I watch him drop
toward a small grove of trees through a winter twilight.
He crashes into branches and lies tangled there, hanging
head down and still.

Southward we move, pounding through the snow
with Lobu guiding us. The only sound I hear are the
Words. From our wings they come, and sweeping back
along the wind they find and comfort me.

A Matter of Honor

Through cracks in the floorboard of an old Chevy truck, I watched a blur of gravel streaming by underneath my feet and thought about whatever twelve-year-old boys thought about in 1951. Baseball, maybe. Or, the still-distant possibility of girls. The dust blew in loose spirals behind us and lay finally upon the grass along the road, long after our passing.

My father drove, looking straight ahead, thinking

Originally published in *The Des Moines Register*, August 20, 1989.

165

of business, a Camel pinched between the first and second fingers of his left hand. I knew the look of him without turning. Blue cap, Osh-Kosh B'Gosh striped bib overalls, clean gray work shirt, wire-rimmed glasses.

At the end of his thin legs, high brown shoes worked the pedals of the truck that took us along the roads of summer. His right hand steered, and when a car or truck or tractor passed us going in the opposite direction, the first finger rose and dropped in the customary Iowa finger-wave.

I rode next to him, in the middle, a seating arrangement influenced by parental concern, since the passenger-side door had a tendency to swing open when we hit especially violent bumps. Larry, the hired man, dealt with the perils of the outside position and told me that chewing Wrigley's Spearmint gum while smoking tasted good.

I used to wonder if Larry might just disappear into the dust sometime, Spearmint gum and cigarette with him, the whirling child of a spring chuckhole wedded to a faulty door latch. But it never seemed to bother him. In those days, you took your risks and danced or fought at the Castle Club in Charles City on Saturday nights.

We were headed northeast out of Rockford toward a farm near Colwell. The Chevy, larger than a pickup and smaller than a grain truck, was loaded with chicken coops stacked high and roped down, cinched tight with the same slipknots I now use to fasten my canoe on car tops. The wire partitions for corraling feathered things that preferred not to be captured rattled between the coops and sideboards.

And wedged securely into the left-hand rear corner of the truck box was the Fairbanks & Morse portable scale. Though the scale was merely an intermediary device for converting poultry into money, the events surrounding it on this day would take the measure of something more than chickens.

We pulled into the farm yard of Ol' Lady Smith's place about eight in the morning. My father called most farm women "Ol' Lady." Age or looks had nothing to do with it. It was his preferred term, one that substituted for "Mrs." or "Miss" or anything else you could conjure up, and he meant no disrespect by the use of it. As for the last name, I am using "Smith" here because I cannot recall her name and wouldn't use it if I did remember.

Larry and I unloaded the scale and coops and catching equipment while my father talked amiably about weather and prices with the fortyish Ol' Lady Smith, sharpening his pencil with a jackknife. We had come to buy 750 leghorn broiler hens on this Wednesday.

I poured water into the sponge of the dust mask my father made me wear. His lungs suffered more from the dust of ten thousand chicken houses than from cigarettes, and he was determined that I would remain pure of breath for the tasks that awaited me in a larger world.

Wading into a large shed with hundreds of frightened, flying, running, screaming chickens is a torment I would reserve only for my enemies. But for eight summers that's what I did.

My father started me out in the back room of our produce house where we warehoused the chickens while waiting for semitrailer trucks that would take them onward to the cities. Sometimes there were thousands of

167

birds back there, locked in what we called "batteries," which were large, rolling units of sixteen cages, five chickens to a cage.

That many chickens produces a fair amount of rather unpleasant output. Therefore, the least-favored task in the business was scraping and shoveling that nastiness into trucks for removal. On my first day of working for him, my father took me to the back room and provided me with a scraper, a shovel, and slender words that have fattened over the years: "Son, you'll always be able to say you started at the bottom." He smiled, touched me on the shoulder, and walked back to his office, while I contemplated the virtues of perdition relative to what I saw before me.

So I began there. After I had suffered long, and in silence, I was promoted to the truck, where the air smelled of country mornings instead of manure, except for the chicken houses where the dust flew and the hard slash of ammonia instantly penetrated the most obscure places in your brain.

Larry and I set up the wire catch pen and drove part of the flock into it. Kneeling down, we grabbed the terrified and flapping hens by the legs, four in each hand, and carried them to the door where my father assiduously put them into the coops. When a dozen or so coops were filled, we went outside to help him weigh them while the Lady Smith watched closely.

Each coop had been weighed empty, with the tare carefully noted. Filled with chickens, the gross weight was observed and the net calculated.

My father checked the accuracy of the scale every

week. And he went even further than that. I had learned how to round in my studies of arithmetic, but he had his own system. For any ounces over a given pound in gross weight, my father rounded up to the next whole pound, which meant the farmers consistently were receiving a large benefit in poundage.

I once asked him why he rounded as he did, for my textbooks instructed otherwise. His response was characteristically direct: "So nobody can ever accuse me of cheating them in the rounding, I always give the farmer the next higher pound, even if the weight is only an ounce over a given pound."

My father cherished his reputation for honest practice and strove to protect it, so I did not press him further, even though I knew his rounding procedures were arithmetically incorrect and financially draining. The trust in his methods was such that most farmers went on with other things while we collected their chickens and never questioned my father's numbers.

We were covered with dust, sweating in the June sun, and had loaded about five hundred of the hens when an event occurred that has stayed with me always. For some reason, Ol' Lady Smith accused my father of shorting her on the weights.

He was bent over the scale but straightened up slowly at her words, the Osh-Kosh B'Gosh bibs hanging from his bony shoulders. His face reddened in the kind of anger I only saw on certain occasions, such as that night when, caught in the frenzied grip of some glandular malfunction, I used my shortstop's arm to fire an apple through the screen door of a town official's home.

My father said nothing. He just looked at the Smith woman, looked at the sky, then looked at Larry and me. "I want you boys to take every goddamn chicken out of those coops, one at a time, very carefully, and put them all back in the chicken house." He closed his weight book with a slap, tucked it into the front pocket of his bibs, shoved his pencil in after it, and lit a Camel.

I was as angry as my father, for I had watched him lean against the currents of dishonesty time after time in his life and business. Larry didn't seem to care one way or the other. It was still four days to Saturday night, and whether we loaded chickens or unloaded them was of little concern to him.

So we put the chickens back into Ol' Lady Smith's chicken house, one by one, and carefully. At about chicken three hundred, she decided she had been wrong in her accusation and said so. My father refused to look at her. "Just keep unloading, boys," he instructed us.

The Smith lady began to apologize fervently. She pleaded with my father to take her broilers. He smoked, said nothing, and began to tie down the stacks of empty coops on the truck. We lifted the Fairbanks & Morse into its place, put the tailgates in their slots, and slid into the truck.

My father was silent all the way back to Rockford. His face was still red, and he worked his jaw back and forth in anger at the undeserved humiliation.

Then the phone calls began. Every night, Ol' Lady Smith would call our home and beg my father to come pick up her chickens. She knew our price was better than she could get anywhere else. You see, we had a contract with a large Milwaukee firm that specialized in supplying various ethnic groups in that city with certain types of food required for holiday occasions.

On Tuesdays, the Milwaukee folks would call and place their order with us: two thousand broiler hens about three to four pounds, six hundred capons, one hundred ducks, and so forth. Because of this custom work, my dad was able to pay higher than the market rate for poultry. He would call around the countryside, locate the needed stock, and make his deal over the phone. So the woman with the broiler hens regretted her spasm there in the dust of an Iowa farmyard, burdened more, I believe, by the threat of pecuniary loss than by any sense of true remorse.

This went on for about a week. Her broilers were growing too heavy for our needs, and she knew it. So did my father. Each evening, he spoke politely to her and said that he was not interested in doing business with her. Then one night, with no advance notice to any of us, he simply told her that we would be there first thing in the morning to get her chickens.

So we loaded Ol' Lady Smith's hens a second time. She chattered around, servile. My father was civil, but distant and cool. He weighed the chickens, wrote her a check out of the long book that said "Waller Produce Company" on the front, and sent Ol' Lady Smith's broiler hens to the ethnic groups of Milwaukee, covered as they were with both feathers and righteousness.

He bought her poultry for years after that and never once mentioned his fury at her accusation, though I knew it rested inside of him like a lump of hot chicken fat. His ultimate revenge was fair profit. He was both practical and principled. He could space the two when his honor was threatened and then close the gap when the time was right.

Matters of ethics and honor are difficult, can become confused and abstruse. You learn about such things not from books, but from example. You learn about them standing on your feet, in the sun outside of Ol' Lady Smith's chicken house, watching your father's face harden, his eyes turning to liquid hydrogen, his voice saying, "I want you boys to take every goddamn chicken out of those coops, one at a time, very carefully, and put them all back in the chicken house."

For honor is hard to come by. And pride that flows from honor is not false. Slowly, implicitly, you begin to understand that. You pick it up riding beside a thin and bony man in striped bib overalls, watching the Iowa roads run backward in time through the cracked floorboards of an aging truck, watching the dust blow in loose spirals behind you before coming to rest, once and finally, upon the summer grass, long after your passing.